GF Press

PUT IT IN THE CHICKEN

A Cambodian Memoir

TV GUY SERIES

GLEN FELGATE

GF Press

Paperback edition ISBN: 978-1-916614-00-0

Hardback edition ISBN: 978-1-916614-01-7

Large Print Paperback edition ISBN: 978-1-916614-02-4

Large Print Hardback edition ISBN: 978-1-916614-03-1

Published by GF Press, 2023

Formatted by Ant Press

CONTENTS

THE FIRST TIME Phnom Penh ever came up in conversation, I was in the departure lounge at Kinshasa airport. I was leaving Africa, having spent four weeks as a journalist covering events in the Republic of Congo – or Congo-Brazzaville as we called it at the time. A civil war had broken out between the Republic's former President Denis Sassou Nguesso, and the country's then-leader President Pascal Lissouba. I was covering the story for my employer, Reuters.

As was usually the case in wars in deepest, darkest Africa, those of us covering the story had banded together. In locations as haphazard, erratic and dangerous as the ones we usually found ourselves in, we preferred safety in numbers. And although in theory and on paper, we were competitors, in reality, we often worked together.

Somehow I had become part of the elite journalistic "merry-go-round" that traipsed in and out of warzones and areas of civil strife with frightening regularity - with frightening being the operative word. Generally, we were a happy-go-lucky lot that took things as they came. As had been the case in Congo-Brazzaville.

However, with the fighting between the challenger Denis Sassou Nguesso and the country's leader President Pascal Lissouba over, the story was considered dead. It was time for us to return to our respective head offices to wait patiently for the next assignment.

With the story covered, we took a dug-out canoe across the river to Congo-Kinshasa to spend a raucously drunken night with our fellow journalists in the Intercontinental Hotel bar before heading off the following day to the airport.

As journalists are wont to do, we took over the bar, filling the place with wine, whisky, banter and song to the point where the hotel's other guests gave us an extremely wide berth. As a result of our endeavours, the next day, I entered Kinshasa Airport's rather simply furnished international departure lounge with a heavy head and a depleted money belt. There, my agency friend and colleague Myles Tierney raised his voice above the din from our fellow travellers to proudly announce his next assignment.

"I'm going to Cambodia! I'm going to Phnom Penh!" And then, in more measured tones, he explained why.

"They found Pol Pot. He's up in a jungle hideout somewhere, and I've got to go find him."

It sounded like an arduous task – but one that I was sure Myles was entirely capable of. After all, as the Associated Press Television News leading man in Africa, he was used to getting himself in - and out of - hard to get to places and situations. And this new assignment was more of the same.

As for Pol Pot, everyone knew him as the notorious, murderous leader of the genocidal Khmer Rouge regime that ruled Cambodia from 1975-1979. His legacy was that he emptied out the country's cities and forced the population into the countryside in a desperate bid to turn the nation into a totalitarian agricultural state. He saw farming as the key to success. He was wrong, and millions died.

But that was then, and this was now. And, now, it seemed, the former dictator had been found in his jungle hideout, and the Cambodians were planning to put him on trial. Whether it was a show trial or not was anyone's guess – and that was presumably what Myles was being sent to Cambodia to find out.

As a journalist, the fact that someone had found Pol Pot and that one of my journalist friends was travelling to Cambodia to cover the story should have made me jealous. However, the truth of the matter was that having spent the last few weeks living on the edge in the Congos, I was happy to take a break. Having said that, I was determined not to rain on Myles' parade. "Wow, that's great!" I lied as we headed for the bar in the departure lounge for a drink.

As it happened, it would be the last drink I would ever have with Myles. It was also the last interaction I would have with him too. He was killed in a checkpoint ambush about a year later while on assignment in Sierra Leone.

Furthermore, Myles never did make it to Phnom Penh. He was stood down by the agency in favour of someone closer to the story. It was a trend that was becoming increasingly common in the late '90s as news became more and more of a business and less and less a public service. Nevertheless, from that moment on, whenever I thought of Phnom Penh, I thought of Myles. And I wondered what he would have thought of me being sent to Cambodia on a permanent assignment to set up a TV channel - for that was my mission.

As for me, I put the blame squarely at the feet of my own wanderlust. After years of traipsing around the world's hotspots, I needed something more permanent. I needed a bureau. I needed roots. Unfortunately, my employers at Reuters did not have a bureau to offer, right when I wanted it. So I took matters into my own hands and headed east on behalf of a start-up that excelled in delivering TV news footage via the internet - something that is all the rage now but wasn't then. I put down roots in Singapore.

At the time, we were seen as upstarts or disruptors, and the roots I put down were soon torn up when the investors got spooked by the dot-com bust. We were out of business, and I was out of a job - left high and dry in the ever-so-pricey Singapore.

With this in mind, I took a job with a pan-Asian sports network producing video news reports and doing voice-overs. They gave me the job on the strength of my radio voice - rather than my sports knowledge.

"We want you on board," Executive Producer Dez informed me as soon as he had heard my voice-over.

"You do realise that the last time I worked in sports Bjorn Bjorg was playing John McEnroe at Wimbledon," I replied. My journalistic frankness coming to the fore.

"Yes, we know," came the reply. "That is why we can only pay you peanuts."

Despite the cut in salary, I took the position. After all, it kept me in Singapore. It kept me in Asia. And, it saved me the embarrassment of heading back to London with my tail between my now lopped-off legs.

Besides, working in a sports newsroom was much like working in a traditional newsroom - but with much less pressure. Unlike a regular newsroom, where orders were barked across desks when copy, script and footage were ready, a sports newsroom had celebratory yelps and hoots when goals were scored, or amazing sporting feats were achieved. And, whereas regular newsroom hacks were studious and somewhat academic in their endeavours, sports journalists were usually always animated 'anoraks'. They were passionate. They knew almost anything and everything about their chosen sport - and nearly every sport, for that matter. They were also a cheerier bunch than the newsmen and newswomen I usually associated with - and a lot less cynical.

And so it was that I found myself sitting amongst people with a passion for all things sporting who could tell you at which precise minute the first goal was scored in FIFA's inaugural 1930s World Cup or how many aces Martina Navratilova served when she won the Wimbledon title in 1982. It was impressive - but it wasn't me. I knew that - and so did my Executive Producer friend, Dez.

The sports job was a stopgap measure until something else came along. So, instead of covering wars and geopolitics, I did sidebar stories about David Beckham's latest haircut or pieces about a surfing dog.

And then, one of my European contacts put me forward for a job in Cambodia - setting up a TV channel. The company was a mobile phone company, and it seemed they had promised a TV Channel to get the licence too.

"He's probably just crazy enough to do it," said my European contact when asked to furnish a name. "Contact Glen".

And so it was after receiving such a glowing recommendation from my European contact, that I found myself sitting in the boardroom of a skyscraper on the waterfront in Singapore. The boardroom had floor-to-ceiling windows, a three-inch shag pile carpet and enough wood panelling to build an entire 50-foot schooner.

"A real live journalist?" the CEO quipped as he strode into the boardroom with his assistant Robert in tow, indicating that he had actually read my CV.

The CEO introduced himself as Yann and explained that he was on the way to New York for an analyst briefing on behalf of the shareholders. He added quickly that he only had an hour to talk because he had to pick up some souvenirs for his wife. He appeared relaxed in jeans and a polo shirt which was a stark contrast to Robert, who entered looking uncomfortably hot in a suit and tie and a shirt with a starched collar to boot.

Meanwhile, Robert sat across the boardroom table from me, mopping his brow with his pocket chief while surreptitiously studying me and taking notes. Their differing styles of dress and manner had me wondering whether this was some bizarre kind of corporate good cop, bad cop routine.

Yann appeared relaxed and trendy. Robert looked fidgety and on edge. I sat and waited for the inevitable trick question. I was sure it would be Robert who would deliver it.

"So, you want to help launch our TV station then, do you?" the CEO asked.

"Well, I've never set up a TV station before," I replied again with journalistic frankness.

"Well, do you want to?" the CEO continued without batting an eyelid.

"Yes," I nodded.

"Good. You need to meet our local partners," and then turning to Robert. "Robert, set it up, please."

With that, Robert's fidgeting became even more pronounced. He then rolled his eyes and nodded. He was clearly displeased with having been ordered to contact the local partner. Yann looked over at me and winked.

"Robert and the local partner don't quite see eye to eye. "What is it he calls you? The nerd? Is that it?" Yann laughed before turning back to me. "I suppose we are all nerds in this industry, aren't we?"

"But, he should like you, though. He likes the media – and anyone that can raise his profile in front of the Prime Minister. Anyway, we will give him his TV channel. By the way, how big do we need to build the studio?"

"About as big as this room," I hesitated and replied. Was it the inevitable trick question to test my knowledge of TV?

"Good," Yann replied. "Now, I have to go shopping. Wife's orders."

Yann went shopping and then jetted off to New York.

Robert went back to his office to grudgingly call the local partner. And I went back to the sports desk.

"We seem to have found you a TV man," I heard Robert announcing down the phone. "We'll send him over soon."

Within a week, I was seated on the early morning Silk Air flight to Phnom Penh, staring down at Cambodia's Tonle Sap River. The river wound its way through the low-rise city and joined with another famous waterway, the Mekong River.

As I sat strapped into my seat, peering at Phnom Penh's famous rivers and sun-scorched landscape, I couldn't help wondering what exactly I was doing there. After all, as I had said, I had never set up a TV station before.

I also couldn't help wondering about my long-lost friend Myles who never quite made it to Phnom Penh.

I wondered about many things as I touched down at Phnom Penh's Pochenthong International Airport on that blisteringly hot April morning.

I OFFICIALLY ARRIVED in Cambodia to start my new job on April 11th, 2002. It was right at the start of the four-day Khmer New Year holiday. That was the owner's idea. He was raring to go. Besides, he didn't believe in holidays. As far as he was concerned, work was a holiday. It was his idea of fun. He was a man of few other interests.

The owner's secretary Lyda picked me up at the airport. As it happened, she was the first Cambodian I had ever met. She had been dispatched to the airport to meet me – and when I arrived, I could see why. It wasn't just that she made a very welcoming first impression for any first-time visitor. Her distinctly Buddhist charm and calm also brought a sense of order to what was otherwise absolute mayhem.

The airport arrivals hall was dusty and chaotic, with crowds gathered in bunches behind the immigration desks. Officialdom at the airport was apparent but extremely lax. I watched as money changed hands between newcomers and officials and wondered how many of the notes being handed over would make their way into official coffers. The haphazard, ramshackle, dusty scene reminded me of airports in Albania and Africa, where I had previously worked as a journalist. I immediately liked what I saw. I felt at home.

"Mr. Glen?"

I looked down to see a wide-eyed, oval-shaped face smiling at me. There was innocence in the eyes, warmth in the smile and calm amidst the chaos. It was just what I needed as I jostled with the throng of fellow travellers.

"I'm Lyda," the lady announced as she clasped her palms together and bowed. "I am here to help you."

"Nice to meet you," I replied, holding out my hand in greeting. It was a Western habit I would soon discard in favour of the dainty, respectful bow known in Cambodian as *som pas*.

"Is this your first time in Cambodia?" Lyda asked.

"Yes, but I have lived in Singapore and Malaysia," I replied.

"Cambodia is different," Lyda said emphatically and proudly. She flashed a cheeky smile and delicately re-arranged her shiny blue-black hair. She then directed her attention to a blue-uniformed immigration official as he approached her. Her voice and stature immediately changed as the official took my passport and papers. She barked some high-pitched commands at the official, who nodded, turned on his heel, and disappeared into the disorderly throng still gathering around the immigration desks. The blue-uniformed official wasted no time in getting to the task at hand. It was apparent that it was Lyda who was calling the shots.

"Do you have children?" Lyda asked out of the blue as she politely turned to me.

"Er...no," I replied. I was somewhat taken aback by her blunt approach to introductory small talk.

"I'm sorry," Lyda replied sadly.

"No, no," I found myself explaining to convince her there was actually nothing wrong with me on that particular front, which is what I thought her response implied. "I'm not married. I have a girlfriend. She is in the UK. We work a lot."

It was true. I did have a girlfriend. She was French and lived in London

Lyda seemed genuinely sorry for me that I had no children. At first, I was bemused. Then it dawned on me that, to an Asian, having children to look after you in your old age was a blessing. Not having children was a curse. Asian offspring were effectively the parents' pension plan – instead of having an official social welfare system. I learned that in Malaysia and Singapore.

"Do you have children?" I added.

"Yes, a boy and a girl," she beamed back at me.

"You're fortunate," I remarked. "They can look after you."

We then stared at each other in silence. I was a novel curiosity to my new host, and she continued to gaze at me unabashedly. She studied me intently, continuing to smile at me all the while.

"Here he comes," Lyda announced, breaking the silence as the official with my passport sauntered over. There followed some sing-song Khmer as Lyda and the official exchanged words. I wasn't quite sure if Lyda was scolding him for taking too long or thanking him for returning so quickly. However, at the end of it, there were bows and thanks followed by the subtle placement of a ten-dollar bill in the immigration official's palm. I was sure that that particular note would definitely not find its way to the tax department.

"Ok, we can go," Lyda said as she turned to me, smiling and gesturing towards the airport's exit. She led the way – not so much walking, strutting, or strolling as gliding. Every once in a while, she turned to check on me, smiling sweetly as she did so. The soldier guarding the exit bowed to Lyda as she passed. There was no doubt that Lyda was a woman of substance – either that or she had connections.

As I studied her further, I noticed that hers was an open, pleasant face with a broad, bright smile. She had a proud, regal disposition. She moved effortlessly, she spoke effortlessly, and she smiled effortlessly. Her smooth, efficient manner accentuated her quiet, gentle confidence. I wondered if her gentle disposition was unique or typical of Cambodian culture.

Lyda was petite and pretty. She had an oval cream-coloured face and wore shoulder-length hair parted in the middle. One length of her immaculately straight blue-black hair hung down the side of her face to her shoulder while the other was tucked behind her ear. She was traditionally yet stylishly turned out. She wore a reddish-brown silk wrap offset by a pink embroidered short-sleeve top.

She strolled daintily out of the terminal building exuding presence every step of the way. As she exited the building, she hoisted a plastic folder to her face to shield herself from the sun's unmerciful rays. She held the makeshift sun shield above her head as she turned to introduce me to our driver.

"This is Mr. Ratanak," Lyda announced. "He is the owner's driver."

"*Sok Sabay*, sir," Mr. Ratanak said, smiling and bowing, offering me peace and happiness in greeting. He stood next to a polished-to-perfection shiny black Toyota Land Cruiser. I bowed in return, and he opened the rear passenger door for me to climb in. He then helped Lyda into the front seat.

"Mr. Ratanak does not speak much English," Lyda explained as Mr. Ratanak took the wheel. "But he drives very well. He is also very safe. Oknha trusts him."

"Oknha?" I replied quizzically.

"Yes, that is the name of an important person in Cambodia," Lyda replied. "He is the owner."

As it happened, *Oknha* was the honorific title bestowed on Cambodians of immense wealth who regularly donated to the ruling party, the CPP (the Cambodian People's Party), of which the prime minister was the head. There were about twenty such *Oknhas* in Cambodia at that time. They were considered the country's elite having an enviable direct line to the prime minister and access to lucrative business licences. The *Oknha* whom Lyda spoke was said to be one of the youngest and most dynamic in the country.

I had first heard of the *Oknha* from Robert in Singapore. The *Oknha* had grand plans to raise his profile in front of the country and even the country's prime minister. He saw this as the key to success, and now he had financial backing from the mobile company. He just needed the influence. The first step would be setting up a nationwide television network. Knowing as he did that television had the most significant impact and reach in Cambodia, Oknha was hoping to create the biggest and best channel in the country to attract the largest audience and grow his influence. He saw this as a way to help the prime minister deliver his all-important public messages and maintain his hold on power. And, of course, with Oknha now being one of the country's elites with access to the necessary licences for the major industries, he wanted to maintain his own position too. Television would be just one of the tools in Oknha's impressive arsenal.

However, while Lyda seemed impressed with Oknha, Robert in Singapore was less so. In fact, he could barely conceal his disdain when he briefed me on the subject of the TV project in his office in Singapore.

"The local shareholder's a real piece of work!" Robert barked at me across the boardroom table. "In a country where it costs just fifty dollars to have someone shot, it's a wonder no one's done it yet!" he continued.

Robert stared at me intently through his wire-framed spectacles perched upon his beak-like nose. He wore a charcoal grey suit and a striped shirt set off by a navy blue paisley tie and matching handkerchief – the tip of which protruded from his suit pocket. He looked somewhat out of place in what appeared to be a Silicon Valley-style Asian hi-tech operation centre. He was overdressed for Singapore's sweltering heat and the casual atmosphere of the skyscraper office. Everyone else looked comfortable and relaxed in polo shirts, faded jeans and moccasins. He looked far from relaxed - and was getting increasingly flustered. He had to calm himself down.

"Never mind! Sometimes...," Robert paused for effect. "Just sometimes...when you work where we work, you must work with some very unsavoury characters."

"Mind you, he does handle the government well. I will

give him that," Robert added as an afterthought. "You'll meet him soon enough."

I was still trying to formulate a picture of this so-called Oknha I was about to meet when Lyda interrupted my thoughts.

"This is Monivong Boulevard. It is our Orchard Road," Lyda announced proudly as we approached the heart of the Cambodian capital Phnom Penh.

I looked around to see the dirt, dust and dilapidation I had seen on Pochentong Boulevard on the way from the airport – but just more of it. There were also more Chinese shophouses but only one hotel and one office block. The office block seemed to be the focal point for the Cambodian capital's central business district, and the boulevard had two lanes on either side of the street and plenty of intersections. It looked more business-like than the other streets I'd seen, but it was certainly no Singaporean Orchard Road.

I had just come from Orchard Road in Singapore. It was awash with high-rise shopping malls with neon lights and plasma screens on every street corner. It was also home to some of the world's glitziest brands and some of Asia's best-heeled high society shoppers. It was a far cry from what I saw before me on this, my first look at downtown Phnom Penh.

Instead, I saw shops with cavernous, dark and dusty interiors before me. The shophouse interiors were unlit and gloomy and, as a result, unwelcoming. I presumed that the lack of lighting was a concession to the city's expensive and unreliable power supply.

Also, the branding was as basic as the presentation. Hand-painted signs that hung haphazardly over shop-front doorways seemed to be the order of the day. They were almost complex in their simplicity.

"SAM TRY MAKE ALL KIND OF STAINLESS STEEL", read one sign (with SAM TRY being the owner's name and not a reference to his effort).

"SHOP FOR SELLING ALL KINDS ELECTRICAL GOOD", read another.

There was absolutely no concern for competition or improving one's sales pitch through positioning or choice of location. Block upon city block of shops sold the same products. As we drove, I contemplated that the Western concept of 'location, location, location' was yet to take hold here in downtown Phnom Penh. But there, again, there were very few Cambodian shoppers to tout their wares to anyway. The shops and the sidewalks that fronted the shophouses were devoid of traffic – pedestrian or otherwise. Those who did have money to shop were doing their rounds in the dusty, cluttered markets I had passed on my way to town from the airport. There, sturdy, weather-worn Cambodian women wearing long-sleeved shirts, baggy dark trousers and floppy hats weaved their way through sagging stalls with makeshift tarps and plastic sheeting as awnings. The Cambodian housewives squeezed fruit, prodded vegetables and barked orders in high-pitched voices at the stall-holders who perched proudly behind their produce. They hid from the sun under their rickety awnings, lifting their hands to shield their eyes from the glare around them as they addressed would-be customers. It was noisy, dusty and chaotic but made for a colourful, lively scene.

By the time I arrived in downtown Phnom Penh proper, I had been on the ground in Phnom Penh for less than an hour. I was getting my first taste of the city. Sitting in the Toyota Land Cruiser's back seat, which appeared to be a vehicle of choice for the city's well-heeled businessmen and entrepreneurs.

As we made our way to the centre of town and beyond, I peered through the tinted glass windows to see all manner of cars and trucks in every imaginable state of destitution and disrepair. There were powder blue Korean flat-bed trucks laden with axle-breaking loads of bricks and cement. Wobbly-wheeled vans made up the country's unofficial bus and taxi network. And then there were the *motos* - the local scooters and motorbikes - that hurtled, ambled, stopped, and started as they made their way along the city's roads and boulevards.

My driver Mr. Ratanak was now carving his way cautiously through the motorized melee. He had achieved a top speed of 30 kilometres per hour. He was in no hurry. He was also careful to avoid hitting one of the city's many baseball-capped *moto* drivers. They were a menace to themselves and everyone around them. They darted to and fro, weaving in and out of lanes, dividers, and oncoming cars. They came to a standing stop wherever they saw fit. At red lights, they gathered in veritable swarms like bees around honey. There they jockeyed for position and edged in front of one another and the waiting cars and trucks. Those too impatient for the lights to change broke away and scampered across busy intersections in defiance of the crossing traffic.

By the time we arrived on Monivong Boulevard in the city's centre, I was a nervous wreck. Mr. Ratanak and Lyda, on the other hand, were the picture of calm. They were oblivious to the chaos.

Juxtaposed with the mayhem outside was the Land Cruiser interior. It was cooled to a comfortable 24 degrees, and a chilled bottle of water sat temptingly tucked into the pocket of the seat in front of me. An English language radio station played the latest Western hits, intermittently broken up by announcements of the channel's call sign, LOVE FM. I listened with interest. As I listened to the music and sat back in my leather-upholstered seat, I felt far removed from the dust, dirt and chaos of the world outside. I felt like I was in a temperature-controlled mobile cocoon.

Yet, despite the neglect outside, there was potential. The houses and villas were stable, sturdy and well-constructed. The Chinese shophouses that lined Phnom Penh's Pochentong Boulevard provided the thoroughfare's only concession to commerce. At the same time, the French colonial villas with their columns, porches, balconies and wooden shutters were a testament to days when Phnom Penh was once known as the pearl of the Orient.

As a former journalist, I knew something of Cambodia's recent past. I, like many others, had heard the horror stories that had come about as a result of the Khmer Rouge regime.

Fortunately, the Khmer Rouge were long gone by the time I arrived in Phnom Penh in that April of 2002. For many, the memories of Khmer Rouge hardship and lost loved ones had been replaced by new anxieties borne of day-to-day survival. After all, Cambodia was still poor, and so were the people. Yet despite the desperate poverty, Phnom Penh's residents appeared to buzz around the city in desperate determination. I could sense the energy.

As I got to grips with my newfound surroundings, Lyda turned to me again.

"We go to see the *Oknha*. He is important," Lyda announced.

As Mr. Ratanak urged the Landcruiser up the ramp leading to the Hotel Cambodiana's main entrance, the significance of the hotel's location on the banks of the Tonle Sap as it joined the Mekong River was not lost on me. It was a fitting backdrop to the start of my new life in Phnom Penh.

"Make sure to call him Oknha," Lyda added.

OKNHA

"So, you know everything there is to know about television in Asia?" the *Oknha* asked.

"No, no, not at all," I replied timidly.

"And you've just flown in from Europe? So, what do you know about Asia?"

"Er...um...no, Oknha," I replied, somewhat confused by Oknha's line of questioning. "I've just come from Singapore. I have been working there for more than a year."

"Mmmhhh, mmm, mmm," the *Oknha* responded dismissively as he eyed me suspiciously.

It had been about thirty minutes since I had been introduced to Oknha, and the meeting wasn't going well at all. In fact, it seemed to be going downright awfully, bearing in mind that I had followed Lyda's instructions to the T and even smiled, bowed, and scraped at every available opportunity. And, yes, I had also called the owner Oknha with monotonous regularity. I even threw in a smarmy compliment mentioning how young he looked to be, an accomplished and successful entrepreneur - and a significant influence in South East Asia.

"Mmmhhh, mmmhhh, mmmhhh," was all I got in return.

It was Lyda who had escorted me to the restaurant at the back of the Hotel Cambodiana, and it was there that I found Oknha huddled in deep conversation with a slim blond-haired Western gentleman. Oknha beckoned to a uniformed bodyguard standing off to his right as I approached. The bodyguard approached gingerly, bowing as he neared the table. He bent down to take instruction. Then Oknha's phone rang.

"Excuse me," the Oknha said apologetically as he picked his phone off the table, stood up, wandered across the restaurant talking, and nodded as he went.

"*Baan...aday...okun*," I heard the Oknha say as he agreed, disagreed and thanked in Khmer whoever it was that was calling him. He was on the phone for about fifteen minutes, giving me time to get my bearings and look around the restaurant. And then, he started in his line of questioning.

The restaurant looked more like a cafeteria than an atmospheric hotel eatery. There were fixed tables and chairs with dirty green upholstery, and a tacky buffet was in the centre of the room.

Even though the restaurant was at the back of the hotel bordering the Tonle Sap River, you could not see the water or riverbank. The hotel's architect had seen to that by placing porthole-style windows high in the restaurant's walls. From where I sat, all I could see was what looked like a ship's funnel protruding into a clear blue sky.

Oknha took another call, and the Westerner engaged me

in conversation with a proper introduction. Until then, Oknha had merely barked questions at me before sauntering off to take his second call.

"You must be Glen," the blond-haired gentleman started, flashing a pearly-white smile as he reached across the table to shake my hand. "I'm Bradley. I'm the country manager."

"Ah, you're that Bradley," I said. The penny had finally dropped as to who this mystery man actually was. "Robert told me about you. I answer to you."

"Yes, I'm in charge of the whole operation - mobile and all," Bradley replied.

Bradley was tall and slim with thick blond hair that topped a pleasant, sun-browned face. His eyes were bright, blue, and honest, and his radiant and infectious smile would put anyone at ease.

"Is that a ship I see out the window?" I took the opportunity to ask Bradley as Oknha continued conversing on the phone.

Yes, it is a ship's funnel," Bradley replied with a grin. "It's a floating casino."

"Casino?"

"Yes, it's a classic Cambodian compromise," Bradley explained. "The casino is on a boat on the river because the government does not want to deal with the violence and crime normally associated with gambling. But they want the revenue and the tourists a casino inevitably brings – from Vietnam, Hong Kong and China. So, they did what they do best. They compromised."

"The casino is owned by a Malaysian gambling company," continued Bradley. "The government said they could move the casino onto a boat on the Mekong River.

That way, the casino can attract those visiting Phnom Penh. Still, it would remain suitably offshore – so they can maintain their dignity. At least, that's the story I was told. It makes sense. You will find that there's a way around most things here."

As Bradley finished the explanation, Oknha returned to the table.

"Sorry, that was the Prime Minister's people again," Oknha mentioned matter-of-factly. "They want me to go with the PM on a trip. So...this TV? Can I tell the PM that it will be on air at the end of the year?"

"Well, that could depend on how big the network is, Oknha? And a few other things...." I started to reply.

"It'll be big. Nationwide," Oknha replied abruptly as if I should have been briefed on that particular point beforehand. "The Nerd should have told you before you came here."

It was the first time I heard Oknha refer to Robert as 'The Nerd.' It wouldn't be the last.

And then Oknha turned to Bradley, "Why are they always looking to cut costs?"

As Oknha spoke, a group of ministers arrived at the restaurant. They had been attending an investment forum upstairs in one of the hotel's conference rooms. They were on their lunch break. There were about thirty of them in total, and they sidled up to us to bow to Oknha. He responded dismissively, barely even looking at them. Instead, he concentrated on his noodle soup.

"Bradley, I'll take it from here," Oknha announced, wiping his mouth with a white linen napkin. "It's time for Mr. Glen to go on the tour. I'll see you and Jean at the party?"

Bradley nodded, "I wouldn't miss it."

"Mr. Glen, you will be there too?" Oknha added.

"Well, I need to....." I began.

"Glen will be there," Bradley said, brandishing his trademark smile and winking at me.

The Oknha's tour of Phnom Penh meant dropping in unannounced on the Minister of Information, sauntering past military checkpoints at various TV and radio stations, and walking unobstructed into the control room of the state broadcaster. All the while, he was giving me a running commentary.

"I was arrested in Thailand," Oknha announced as he chewed on a stick of gum. "I crossed the border with my brother in the days of the Khmer Rouge, and we got arrested. Then we were released and put in a refugee camp. My parents had already died many years ago. They were killed by the Khmer Rouge for being too Chinese."

With that, Oknha gave a slight pause. As he did so, our driver came to a sudden halt. Suddenly the two camouflage-clad motorcycle outriders accompanying us on our town tour now leapt off their bikes, un-holstered their pistols and began moving the crowd, circling a downed motorbike. The *moto* was now lying in the middle of the road, its wheels still spinning. The bystanders stepped back as they saw Oknha's bodyguards and the weaponry they now menacingly held aloft.

"Do they know how to use those things?" I asked, only

realising what I had said once the words were out of my mouth. Oknha looked at me intently. And then he laughed.

"Mr. Glen, you really are a *Barang*, aren't you?"

"Sorry, Oknha? What am I?"

"*Barang*...foreigner...a pointy nose foreigner," Oknha explained. "It's what we call you foreigners here. In fact, I'm practically a *barang* myself. I have an Australian passport."

As it happened, Oknha had been rescued from the refugee camps by his uncle and then taken to Australia. There he had been brought up by his sister. He was schooled there and worked there. He worked until 1992 when the United Nations established Cambodia's United Nations Transitional Authority. With the arrival of UNTAC - as the UN body became known - Oknha saw his chance. After all, he could speak English and Khmer and was familiar with Western ways. He knew he would be in demand if he returned to his homeland. He started with office supplies, selling printers and photocopiers and the like. Now he was one of the wealthiest *Oknhas* in the country with his own mobile phone network, parcels of land and other commercial interests. He was doing what he wanted to do - helping to rebuild his country. Soon, he would have his own television network to tell everyone how far he had come. Making it a success would be my responsibility.

"And what about those people back there with the bike?" I asked after the bodyguards had remounted their own motorbikes, and we went on our way.

"Them?" he asked, looking like he had already moved on from what he considered a typical, commonplace incident on the streets of Phnom Penh. "A robber had stolen a *moto* and that crowd had chased him down and dragged him off the bike. They would have beaten him to death had they had their way. It's their only way. We have few police, and those we do have just hide under trees and step out to fine you for some motoring misdemeanour when they want money. It usually happens at the end of the month when they've spent their salary. Otherwise, they do little. The PM is trying to sort that out, though."

"And why did it involve your bodyguards?" I asked.

Again, Oknha stared at me intently before grinning.

"I'm not sure it would be a good idea to let you witness a lynching on your first trip to Cambodia," Oknha laughed.

I smiled back. I was beginning to get Oknha's cheeky sense of humour, which was down-to-earth and Australian. I also felt that he genuinely wanted to help his country get back on its feet. I studied him more closely - or as close as possible without appearing rude.

For a multi-millionaire, he dressed casually. He obviously wore what he wanted – and what made him feel comfortable. On this particular day, Oknha wore dark Brioni slacks – without the matching jacket - and an open-necked white silk shirt, juxtaposed by cheap plastic flip-flops.

Standing at just 5'3", Oknha's height and round, jovial face gave him a youthful, boyish air. He also had a mischievous endearing smile and a quick wit that I would later see him use to charm his would-be business partners and suitors.

And then there was the voice. A distinctly Australian twang formed phrases that included all the latest Western slang. It was somewhat disarming to hear such a broad Australian accent from such a distinctly Asian face. At first, it took some getting used to.

During our drive around town, Oknha's attitude towards me softened noticeably. I was starting to believe that the irritable restaurant episode was for Bradley's benefit. After all, Bradley was the joint venture partner's man. Oknha probably wanted to send a message back to Robert and Yann that when it came to Cambodia, he was calling the shots, not the pale-faced executives sitting in air-conditioned towers in Singapore or Europe. As such, Oknha would decide who would work in Cambodia, who would run his television channel and not them. That I had learned already.

"So, see you at the party tonight," Oknha said, smiling. He didn't bother to bow like Lyda and the other Khmers. Instead, he waved casually as he stuck another stick of chewing gum in his mouth. Oknha then turned to his driver and issued an instruction in Khmer before driving off down the city's dusty, pot-holed roads.

A MAN OF MANY TALENTS – AND SHIRTS

It was Bradley and his wife Jean who picked me up. It was about seven in the evening, and the traffic on Norodom Boulevard in the town centre was light and getting lighter. It was a complete contrast to earlier in the day when I took the opportunity to explore Phnom Penh's famed Russian Market. Then it had been busy as *motos*, Toyota Camrys, and SUVs jostled one another in the narrow streets around the market.

The Russian Market was near the town centre and owed its name to the Russian expats who populated Phnom Penh in the 1980s. At that time, Russians made up most of the foreigners living in Phnom Penh. And, of course, they did much of their shopping in what would become their legacy – the Russian Market.

When I first visited the market on that blisteringly hot weekday afternoon, there were few Russians but a smattering of tourists. The Russians were replaced by T-shirt-clad Western backpackers hunting for unique souvenirs and cheap internationally-branded clothes like The Gap, Levis, Colombia or Ralph Lauren. The clothes were stacked in high piles, and you had to peer over them to speak or even see the stallholders as they sold their wares. And if you wanted to buy a pair of jeans or a designer shirt, there was no trying on any garments because there were no changing rooms or private areas. In fact, there weren't even any mirrors. To gauge how something looked, once on, you would have to guess or rely on the word of your partner, fellow traveller or even the distinctly biased stallholder trying to sell you their wares.

"Mister, look very handsome!" would be the enthusiastically cheeky refrain from behind the stacks of clothes. "Special price for you!"

Simply put, the clothes had been stolen from a local factory. So, woe betide you if you got the size or choice of colour wrong. There would simply be no refund or exchange - ever. No matter how much you pled with or badgered the stallholders. And with this in mind, you could only hope that the sizes on the labels corresponded to those on the garments themselves. If they didn't, too bad.

Despite their hot, humid and cramped conditions, the market stallholders were a cheery and cheeky lot. They traded jokes and banter with one another. They threw provocative comments at tourists as they wandered up and down, mopping sweat from their own hot, dusty brows. They moved carefully and precisely in sauna-like conditions. They sat behind or next to their wares, propping their weary heads up with their hands.

"Buy T-shirt, Sir," one called out to me.

"Have size for you," cried another.

"Where you from?" another stallholder asked, trying to engage me in conversation.

"England, but I came here from Singapore," I replied to this particular line of questioning.

"Singapore is very rich," the stallholder remarked with evident admiration. "Have many tall buildings."

It was a simplistic view of the world, but one that I would hear time and time again. Singapore was the model city that many Cambodians aspired to. It also belied the inferiority complex that was Cambodia's in 2002. Whenever I mentioned Singapore or almost any other Asian capital, there seemed to be a noticeable sigh that signified a certain longing that their country would reach the dizzying heights of their ASEAN neighbours.

In voicing his admiration, this particular stallholder was not alone. Others had said much the same. It was a philosophy unique to Cambodia and the country's tragic history. It was a philosophy I could see in the desperation of the vendors and sellers who sat perched on their stools in the Russian Market.

"All of us Cambodians have friendly faces. But that doesn't mean we should be taken advantage of – as has been the case in the past," a Cambodian friend later explained to me. "They talk about the Thai smile. But really, they should be talking about ours. After all, it is we who have endured. We have experienced the horrors of war - a terrible war. The Thais have never had war. But still, we smile. You look around, and you will see us all smiling. We smile through our hardship and poverty and our unfortunate lot in life. See? We will endure, no matter what. We already have. So, remember...never look down on Cambodian people. Never."

I wandered around the Russian Market and traded good-natured banter with men and women selling jeans, shorts, trinkets and fake watches. They were hot and sweaty in the rabbit warren of a market but appeared happy and content. They seemed entirely satisfied with their lot in life - as simple as it was.

Outside on the street near the Russian Market was a wet market where the Khmers did their own shopping. There, the same stout, weather-worn Cambodian women I had seen on the drive into town from the airport were going about their business, picking vegetables, fruits, and meat for the evening meal. They, too, traded jokes and banter. They, too, appeared happy with their lot.

"Everyone seems genuinely happy," I told Bradley and Jean that night as we headed to *Oknha's* party.

"They're lovely people," Jean agreed. "When you get to know them, they can't do enough for you."

Bradley and Jean had been in Phnom Penh for over two years and as such, had become a fixture on the Phnom Penh expat scene. They also were accepted by the Khmers. They had an easy-going, down-to-earth manner that made them easy to relate to.

"But you wouldn't want to cross any of them," Bradley chimed in with words of caution. "Especially the top ones, the big guys. 'Face' is everything to them. Just ensure nobody loses face, and you'll be fine."

Driving through the town centre, I noticed the streets

were almost empty, except for the occasional moto with a Westerner dangling off the back.

"Where is everybody?" I asked. "They've all disappeared."

"They don't go out much after dark," Jean explained. "They have a saying that 'any Khmer out after eight is probably a no-good Khmer'."

"That sounds a bit harsh," I replied.

"It was the same when we were in Africa," Bradley explained. "Being out after dark is considered dangerous, and if you risk it, you may be up to no good. They think the same here."

Bradley had just finished talking as we turned off Norodom Boulevard into the grounds of an ornate-looking house. Guards scrambled to open and close the ten feet high gates as they ushered Bradley's car off to the side of a loose-gravel car park. Bradley had elected to drive himself so his driver could have the evening off.

As Bradey pulled up, I noticed that there was already a collection of Land Cruisers and other assorted four-wheel drives lined up neatly in a row. There were also about 100 *motos* in a cordoned-off area that was being watched over by a uniformed guard.

"This is one of Oknha's many houses," Bradley explained. "We call it a wedding cake because there are so many layers and rooms."

"Impressive," was all I could think to say.

"Remember to call him Oknha," Bradley reminded me as he got out of the driver's seat.

"I know, I know," I said, smiling.

Oknha had made his way across the massive forecourt past more than 100 tables clustered around an ornamental fountain at their centre. The tables had been laid out on the driveway and were now filled with Khmer ladies in colourful silk wraps and embroidered tops and men in starched white shirts and dark slacks. They were the mobile phone company's employees and had gone home early to prepare for Oknha's party. For many, it was the annual event of the year. After all, it was getting near Khmer New Year, and it was time to celebrate the past year's achievements.

"Bradley, Jean, so happy to see you," Oknha said, smiling as he held his palms together and bowed. "And Mr. Glen, welcome."

Oknha turned to his assistant, Mr. Bunthoeun and gestured towards us.

"Top table, please, Mr. Bunthoeun," Oknha said in English for our benefit. He wanted us to know that we were guests of honour.

"I think he likes you, Glen," Bradley whispered as we followed Mr. Bunthoeun to our place.

Mr Bunthoeun was Oknha's sidekick. He was well-dressed with a short sleeved, button-down shirt, slacks and a well-groomed haircut. He also had a Western outlook. Some said he was qualified as a doctor. He weaved his way through the tables scattered across the drive. There were about one hundred of them, and all of them were full - and segregated. The women sat with women, and the men sat with men. The women wore silk skirts in yellows, pinks, purples and orange with matching embroidered tops. The men wore white shirts and dark slacks. And while the women sat at their tables picking at their food and chatting demurely, the men stood around their tables clinking their glasses in cheers and knocking back whiskies and beers.

Occasionally, a cry would go up as one of their number downed a whisky in one.

"Looks like they're having fun," I remarked to Bradley.

"For now," Bradley said. "Wait until later. They'll all be disappearing into the toilet. It happens every time."

A pretty Cambodian lady approached me as we followed Mr. Bunthoeun to our table.

"Hello, Mr. Glen," she said sweetly as she bowed. "I'm glad you could join us."

I was convinced that I had never seen her before, and I was momentarily lost for words. I had no idea who this was that was greeting me. I wondered how she knew me.

"Ah, hello, Lyda," Jean said, coming to my rescue.

"Lyda?" I said, somewhat taken aback. "I didn't recognise you."

"You look lovely," Jean interjected again, coming to my rescue before I embarrassed myself.

"Thank you," Lyda replied shyly. "Mr. Glen, please join us on the dance floor later."

"Of course," I said, recovering from my surprise and awkward small talk.

"I really didn't recognise her, Jean. She picked me up from the airport, but now she looks different," I said, turning to Jean as we approached our table. "I really had no idea who she was at first."

"I know," Jean agreed. "She's Bradley's PA - and Oknha's. We think she looks so much better without all that makeup."

"Why so much?" I asked.

"We think it's because they want lighter skin," Bradley said, joining the conversation as we took seats.

As soon as we sat down, jugs of Angkor Beer appeared.

Ice was plopped into an Angkor Beer mug at my elbow, and beer was poured on top. I took a couple of swigs and placed the mug back on the table. No sooner had the beer mug been placed on the tabletop when another waiter appeared with another jug of beer and topped it up. This happened for the best part of an hour. I had my own personal 'beer butler' at my absolute beck and call – even more so because he would refill my glass upon every sip, whether I liked it or not. Apparently, he had his orders.

"Careful," Bradley warned, shouting above the music. "It's very easy to lose track."

"I know you haven't been here long, but what do you think of Phnom Penh?" Jean asked, raising her voice above the noise.

By now, the party had started in earnest, and a Cambodian lady had taken to the stage to wail out the latest Khmer hits. She was joined by a drummer, guitarist and keyboard player. The music was high-pitched and somewhat unrefined but had a catchy chorus and beat. The music was so loud that the fabric of my loose-fitting shirtsleeves shivered in time with the domineering bass.

"I like it," I shouted back at Jean. "It has real charm. Not what I expected."

And it was true. Phnom Penh was not at all what I had expected. I had expected to find a city living in fear. I had expected to see people scarred by what they had been through with the Khmer Rouge and the violent elections that followed. Instead, I found people who seemed happy but straightforward and genuinely appreciated their newfound freedoms.

"They have an amazing attitude," I continued. "Especially considering what they have been through."

Both Bradley and Jean nodded in agreement as they sipped their drinks.

I looked around the party to see ordinary Cambodians lost in lively conversation, with women laughing and giggling and the men doing their utmost to get as drunk as they could as fast as they could. The ear-splitting music added to the din and provided a chaotic sound-track to the sing-song revelry.

People were still arriving even though the party was in full swing. Pretty young Cambodian girls continued to arrive in groups of twos, threes and fours, smiling and giggling as they came. They were obviously conscious of the transformation their makeup, hair-styling and traditional silk and lace costumes had upon their appearance, and they complimented one another shyly. Each and every group arrived rich with colour. Reds, oranges, shocking pinks, and purples interspersed with gold and silver embroidery. For the women, there appeared no place for anything dull and down to earth like blacks, browns, and any hues remotely resembling the colours of the earth.

Conversely, the men also came pouring in, looking calm and composed. They also arrived in groups, trading good-natured jibes with one another in cheery greeting. They wore their best silk shirts or immaculate office attire consisting of spotless white shirts and black trousers. They immediately sat at the circular tables and waited for the food, jugs of beer and bottles of whisky.

No one, it seemed, stood on ceremony. No one waited for friends or fellow party guests to take their seats or be served.

Everyone began eating when the food arrived, and they ate without conversation or even looking up at their fellow diners. There would be time for chatter, banter and boozy cheering at the meal's end when everyone had had their fill.

With all the tables now full, the music suddenly stopped. Oknha stepped onto the stage, took the microphone from the lead singer, and started speaking in Khmer.

"He's wearing a different shirt to the one he had on before," I said to Bradley. "Did he spill something?"

"No," Bradley laughed. "It's customary. It's a sign of wealth and importance. He'll probably change once an hour."

"They do the same at weddings," Jean explained.

As Oknha spoke, white-jacketed waiters zeroed in on us every few minutes bearing jugs of beer and buckets of ice. Bradley and I continued to drink beer, and Jean sipped wine.

"...and I'd like to thank Mr. Glen, who is here to help build Cambodia's first nationwide commercial television channel," I heard Oknha say. "Please stand up, Mr. Glen."

I did as I was asked and was greeted by waves of good-natured applause.

"Mr. Glen is a famous journalist," Oknha continued.

And with that, the Khmers cheered once again. Many beamed over at me.

"...and thank you to Mr. Bradley and his lovely wife Jean," Oknha continued. "He will ensure that we have the best mobile phone company in the country."

Oknha returned to his native Khmer. He cracked a few jokes, getting the now somewhat inebriated audience on his side, and then turned to invite the band back on stage. However, instead of handing over the microphone to the lead singer, he held it to his chest, looked up at the stars that shone in the pitch-black Cambodian night sky and then started to sing. The Khmer audience went wild, cheering him on and helping him with the words. Oknha smiled as he strutted around the stage, belting out the chorus. Bradley and Jean stood up and clapped, and I followed suit.

"Is it always like this?" I asked Bradley.

"Not always – but often," Bradley replied.

I was still standing when Lyda came over to our table, bowed and ushered me toward the dance floor just before the stage. Oknha saw me step onto the square parquet dance floor and nodded approvingly.

"See? Mr. Glen is already learning our customs..." Oknha announced into the microphone, and another cheer went up. Once again, I looked up to a sea of beaming faces. The warmth was genuine, and the affection was apparent in everyone I saw.

No sooner had we taken our place on the dance floor did Oknha again relinquish the limelight to the band. They reduced the tempo and started playing a traditional rhythmic number. The thirty or so people on the dance floor regrouped, forming themselves into a circle and began sashaying in an anti-clockwise direction around the floor. They shuffled gracefully in a large circle as they moved their hands with open palms and outstretched fingers, making gentle circular movements in time to the music. I tried to move in time with those around me but in vain. Despite the dance's apparent simplicity, I found it took more work than it looked. I had to resist the urge to dance 'properly' - or at least my version of properly, anyway.

Once the song ended, I bowed to Lyda and weaved back to the table. By that time, Oknha had joined us. He was wearing yet another shirt. He also had some of his Khmer friends in tow.

"This is the Prime Minister's nephew," Oknha said, introducing me to a young Khmer man with a boyish face. "He would like to drink with you."

A tumbler of whisky was placed in my hand, and the Prime Minister's nephew clinked my glass, stared intently into my eyes, and drained his drink in one.

"I don't usually drink Scotch," I said meekly before feeling a sharp jab in my ribs. I turned to see Mr. Bunthoeun smiling at me intently.

"This is the Prime Minister's nephew," Mr. Bunthoeun repeated the introduction as he smiled and nodded animatedly at me.

I got the hint.

"Oh, yes, of course. Cheers, your Excellency," I said, draining my glass.

Oknha once again nodded approvingly before moving off to another table. Bradley, Jean and I resumed our places. I picked up the wine bottle in the centre of the table. It was a Chateau Pavie, Saint Emilion Grand Cru.

"This is a good wine," I remarked. "It costs a few hundred dollars. They must spend a fortune on these things," I said, turning to Bradley.

"They don't. We do," Bradley replied. "This will appear as an expense. I'll end up paying for this."

"Besides, this isn't even that expensive," Jean said, joining in. "You should see it when the rest of the Prime Minister's family is here. The whisky costs thousands, and you can hardly find the entrance for flower baskets and gifts. This is fairly low-brow in comparison. You should see their weddings."

"Yes, but at weddings, they get their money back," Bradley remarked, putting down his iced beer.

"How's that?" I asked.

"Well, you pay on the way out. You get given an envelope, and you're expected to contribute when you leave," Bradley explained.

"Yes, and everyone leaves almost straight after the meal," Jean added. "And I was told by a Khmer lady that how much you give depends on how good the food is."

"That's a bit cavalier," I remarked. "What happens if you get food poisoning? Do you get your money back?"

Bradley laughed, and Jean pulled a face.

Bradley was still laughing when Oknha returned to our table. He stood and cheered us before vanishing once again inside the massive house. Oknha reappeared wearing a crisp, clean, silk orange shirt and headed straight to the dance floor. After a few dances with his staff, he returned once again.

"Welcome to Cambodia, Mr. Glen," Oknha said as he clinked my beer glass with his wine glass before hoisting it to his lips. "Welcome to the team."

JONNO

AFTER MY INITIAL WELCOME, it was straight down to business. To begin with, I spent quite a lot of time with Oknha as we searched for land for the TV channel studios and offices. He would come to pick me up in one of his many cars. Sometimes it would be a Mercedes driven by himself, and at other times it would be the Land Cruiser driven by his driver Mr. Ratanak. We would invariably look at a parcel of land - for better or worse.

"What do you think?" the owner asked as he gave a magnanimous sweep of his hand toward what looked like a flooded rice paddy.

"It's a bit watery," I replied hesitantly. No sooner had I said it when I heard Mr. Buthoeun utter a loud throaty cough. I turned to see Mr. Bunthoeun staring at me with the same intensity he had shown when I had tried not to drink with the Prime Minister's nephew at the party.

"It's the general's land," he whispered urgently.

Luckily the square-jawed general did not appear to

understand English. Oknha spoke a few pleasantries to the general, and then we took our leave.

"He didn't look like a general," I said in my defence as we clambered back into Oknha's car. "He was dressed for golf."

"They all play golf," Bunthoeun replied. "They play with the ministers. They usually lose if they know what's good for them."

Our next stop took us to a plot of land on Pochentong Boulevard up towards the airport.

"What about this?" Oknha asked as we stood talking to a Khmer lady weighed down by sparkling jewellery.

"It's a bit noisy," I replied. "It's right on a busy highway - and it is near the airport."

Once again, Mr. Bunthoeun coughed. And once again, I turned to see Mr. Bunthoeun glaring at me.

"She's a *Lok Chumteav*," Mr. Bunthoen whispered urgently. "It is the equivalent of an *Oknha*!"

Once again, Oknha took his leave of the *Lok Chumteav*, bowing as he did so.

"I didn't know she was important," I said apologetically. "She was dressed like a secretary - a very well-paid secretary."

"She's a government head of protocol," Mr. Bunthoeun responded stoically. "She has to look the part."

Next, we arrived at a plot some 6 kilometres out of town, resting on the riverbank next to the Tonle Sap. It was fronted by a main road to the front and backed onto the Tonle Sap's muddy brown waters at the rear. It measured some 2000 square metres - enough for a studio and offices.

"Who does this belong to?" I asked timidly.

"Another *Oknha*," Mr. Bunthoeun replied, smiling and nodding. His disdain had now been replaced by approval acknowledging that I had finally cottoned on.

"Ah," I replied knowingly.

"It looks perfect," I announced forcefully without even being asked.

My *Oknha* smiled - as did the other *Oknha*, the land's owner.

As it happened, the land wasn't perfect in the slightest. In fact, it was far from perfect. It was right under a major flight path which meant that the noise of the aircraft could affect our sound quality. Also, being next to the river, it stank of the dried fish paste the Khmers called *prahok*, which they make at the end of the rainy season.

Nevertheless, Oknha took it. He relished the fact that he now had even more ties to important people. He was cementing his position and securing his future at the head office's expense.

Having found the land to house the studio building and the transmission tower, it was time to start recruiting.

My priority was finding a broadcast engineer to help build up our nationwide transmission network. My first port of call was Singapore, where I knew of several exceptionally well-qualified broadcast engineers. One, in particular, caught my eye. His name was Donald, and he was a Singaporean-Indian with overseas experience. I invited him over to Phnom Penh to have a look-see. He arrived just after Khmer New Year.

Arriving as he did on a Friday afternoon, I introduced Donald to Oknha and then Bradley. I also showed him our newly acquired land and the mobile phone office I was working out of. He liked what he saw.

However, I didn't count on the fact that Donald was a Bible-bashing Christian who preferred to spend his leisure time in church and meditation - not propping up the bar with a bunch of beer-swigging Aussies, which was somewhat par for the course in 21st-century Cambodia. So he wasn't impressed when I took him to a local bar after work to meet some of the local expat crowd. He also wasn't impressed that a couple of the Aussies got into a set-to that ended up with the American bar owner throwing everyone out - including the two protagonists. By this time, most of them and I were all pretty drunk and ready to go to the next venue. Our two outback brethren had made their peace and encouraged everyone to head to another bar in the town centre. Donald and I tagged along. Donald and I got a lift with one of the other mobile phone employees, who decided to race his colleague in another car. We hurtled at 100 mph along Phnom Penh's near-empty boulevards. We arrived at the next bar at about 11 pm. Donald was looking a bit shaken - to say the least, even at that stage of the evening.

By the time we had finished drinking, it was about midnight. Donald didn't complain about the expat scene or about the fact that it was very late at night. In fact, he had nothing to say at all as one of my expat colleagues raced along in the direction of his hotel. He still didn't say anything as we parted ways, and he went up to his room. He also didn't say anything the following day when I called him from reception to fetch him. I then found out – to my horror – that he had nothing to say during and after the events of the night before because he had already made up his mind about his involvement – or lack thereof – in our TV project. He wanted none of it. He had already booked his ticket home.

"You be careful," was what Donald did say when I took him to the airport to get his flight back to Singapore.

Over the next few days, I tried calling Donald at his Singapore home. At first, there was no answer. And then, on the third day, Donald's teenage son answered the phone.

"Dad's in Afghanistan," the teenager explained. "He'll be back in a few weeks."

"Afghanistan?" I replied quizzically.

"Yes, he is working with one of the TV agencies there, helping with their satellite feeds," Donald's son explained.

And that was that. Donald seemed to think it safer to be working in war-torn Afghanistan than it was to be part of our TV station set-up in Cambodia. I gave up trying to woo Donald and started looking for a new candidate. This time I was determined to find someone made of sturdier stuff. I eventually opted for an Aussie, thinking that an Australian engineer would have plenty of company in downtown Phnom Penh and would be more suited to his compatriots' particular brand of socialising.

It took me a few weeks, but I finally ended up with Jonno. He was an RF engineer from Tasmania with plenty of experience with mobile phone companies and TV stations. He made a living out of building and climbing towers and already had some experience working in Asia. He was, to my mind, ideal.

After weeks of negotiations, Jonno stood waiting for me at Pochentong International Airport dressed in cargo pants shorts and Blundstone work boots. He wore a short-sleeved Columbia work shirt with plenty of pockets. A yellow tower-climbing safety harness was drooped over his shoulder.

As for appearances, he looked like he had come straight from the outback. He was heavyset with thick, curly, unkempt hair and a beer belly that drooped over his belt. His speech matched his appearance and demeanour.

"Strewth, mate. I thought you'd forgotten me," he started. "Anyway, g'day mate. How ya going?"

I gave Jonno a brief overview of the project and who we were being employed by and asked if he had any questions.

"How are the restaurants?" he asked.

"Good," I replied. "Especially if you like French food."

"What about Happy Herb's Pizza?"

"That's the marijuana place, right?"

"Yeah, mate," Jonno replied, giving me a wink. "It's got a cool rep?"

"I wouldn't know," I replied. "I haven't been there."

Although I had never been there and never tried a Happy Herb's Pizza, I was aware of it. Everyone was. Everyone knew someone who had been rendered helpless by the marijuana-laden Happy Herb's pizza. And for those who just wanted to score some weed, there was the 'Happy

Herb's Special' (basically marijuana without the pizza, served as sprigs of marijuana in a bag).

Happy Herb's had a reputation that preceded its very mention. It was celebrated – or infamous – depending on which side of the liberal fence you were on. It was well-known to travellers and tourists alike - especially backpackers. It was also listed in all the major guidebooks. Although the establishment was a mere hole in the wall, located on the riverside's Sisowath Quay, it had come to epitomise Cambodia's free and easy, laid-back culture and, to a certain extent, the country's somewhat lax and lawless ways.

In Happy Herb's defence, it did serve pizza. But it also served weed. It just happened that most of the establishment's clientele went there for the pot – not the pizza dough or the sauce. Nevertheless, Happy Herb's had become an institution, and for some, like Jonno, a trip to Phnom Penh wouldn't be the same without it.

As it happened, two of my friends had Happy Herb's Special pizza one night. It was smothered in marijuana. After scoffing the whole lot down, they were so stoned that instead of going home, they stumbled across the street and threw themselves on a pile of garbage opposite the bar they were drinking in. They slept there all night and woke up stinking of rotten fruit and vegetables. But they swore that that was the only after-effect they ever suffered.

I told Jonno the story as we made our way into town.

"It's an acquired taste and habit, mate," was all he said.

Despite his leanings towards marijuana-laden pizzas, I was impressed that Jonno got straight to work. He knew his stuff, and within a couple of weeks, he had a transmission plan complete with tower locations and suggested transmitter sizes. He also got on pretty well with the city's other Antipodean residents. And for this, I was grateful. It meant that I wouldn't have to babysit him. His downtime was his own, and he made the most of it by getting stoned and imbibing in the local watering holes. I left him to it.

SVEN

Since I had arrived, head office had been poking their nose into everything. They had even dispatched an executive who checked all my business, staffing, and overall start-up plans.

"This TV's going to bleed money!" the executive exclaimed. "You need to get some outstanding salespeople in there! No! I'll get you some people!"

He came up with Sven the Swede. Sven was a Swede who had male model looks. He was tall, dark and handsome and had a clear complexion that came from living and working in Sweden and being brought up on a traditionally Scandinavian diet. With an athletic build and a relaxed manner, Sven would be good at sales. The merest hint of a smile would get any female Sales Executive swooning and signing on any dotted line. Even I had to admit that the executive's instincts were right on this occasion.

When Sven arrived, I was tied up in an advertising agency meeting sorting out our marketing plan, so I asked Jonno to pick him up from the airport. It was a hectic time in town because of a Buddhist congress. Roads were closed, and Phnom Penh's typically light traffic was at a standstill.

"G' day mate", Jonno interrupted my marketing meeting. "Can't find the hotel, mate. It's a nightmare out here. Don't think we'll be getting to his place anytime soon."

"OK, well, I have some spare rooms at the back of my house. Put him there for tonight," I offered.

My house was an old colonial-style building with a kitchen and maid quarters separated from the main block. The primary residence housed my bedroom, a 2nd bedroom, a living room and a dining room, and then there was a guesthouse. The guesthouse was large and consisted of 2 upstairs bedrooms, a downstairs kitchen and a large laundry room. A garage was off to the side – where the previous tenant's guards sometimes slept. A covered patio joined the guesthouse to the main building, and steps led up to the guesthouse bedrooms. It was like having a standalone house at the back of one's home. It was ideal as guest quarters, and it would certainly do to put Sven up for a night or two.

The following day I introduced Sven to some of the local staff. He got along well with the Cambodians and the local expats. All appeared to be going well.

After a day of showing Sven around the office and Phnom Penh, I then left him with Jonno. I had a pre-arranged dinner appointment with Bradley and Jean. Earlier in the week, Bradley had told me that Jean thought I looked extremely stressed and needed a home-cooked meal. She insisted I come round for dinner - and so I did.

Having spent a delightful evening with Bradley and Jean, playing Trivial Pursuit with their teenage son and daughter, I arrived home at midnight – not so late by Cambodia's social standards. I greeted my guard Seila at the gate and asked if our houseguest Sven had returned yet. He hadn't, Seila informed me. I switched on the TV and caught up on world news courtesy of the BBC.

Within about an hour, I heard the gate slide open and clatter shut. It was a bulky metallic contraption measuring about 10 feet in height and always creaked, groaned and clunked as it opened and closed.

'Hello, Sir." I heard Seila say with his customary politeness.

I then heard the front door fly screen fling violently open and slam shut. The frame rocked on its hinges with the force of the abrupt action. And then I saw the dishevelled-looking figure of Sven as he stood swaying near the doorway, staring vacantly past me. He pointed at me aggressively while trying to maintain his balance.

"What about my contract?!" he asked with a Swedish sing-song lilt. "Where's my contract!?"

At first, I thought he was drunk and joking.

"Well, you've had a good night," I laughed, thinking I would humour him.

"What about my contract?!" he demanded once again, aggressively.

It was then that I noticed his clothes. His jeans were torn at the knees, and his elbows poked through holes in his shirtsleeves.

"Have you been in a fight?" I asked. By this time, I was starting to get worried.

At this time, I also heard a woman's voice at my back door. It came from the covered patio bordering the guesthouse.

"Hello!" she cried. She had an Australian twang.

"Yes, can I help?" I replied as I poked my head out of my back door uncertainly. I was becoming bewildered with all this coming and going.

"I am an Australian nurse," she replied. "We found him wandering around in the middle of the road by himself. He was in the middle of the traffic. We picked him up and found this address scribbled on this paper. Is he in the right place?"

"Well, yes. He is staying here. He is a house guest staying up there," I replied, pointing at one of the first-floor guesthouse rooms.

"He's on speed. Have you ever had an experience of dealing with someone on speed?" she asked matter-of-factly.

"Er, no, I can't say I have," I replied.

"Just keep an eye on him and give him plenty of water," she advised. Then, she turned on her heel and walked across the patio and down the drive to her SUV and evening companions. She had done her part.

"What about the contract?" Sven asked as soon as the Australian nurse had left. By this time, he was sitting on a rattan chair in front of the TV. He was rocking back and forth.

"Do yourself a favour Sven, drink some water," I replied, handing him a bottle.

"What about the contract?" came the reply.

This went on for the best part of an hour – Sven questioning me about his contract and me telling him that he was in no fit state to talk about anything. At one point, he demanded to speak to Robert in Singapore.

"Why should I have all the fun?" I said aloud as I pulled

out my mobile phone and dialled Robert. "Here, speak to Robert."

Unfortunately for me, and luckily for Robert, the call went straight to voicemail.

"I am in a reality TV show, and it is going to be on air next year," Sven said. "What about my contract?"

"I am sure you will do very well," I replied again, trying to humour him.

Sven then launched into a monologue, telling me he was being chased and had to reach the top of the mobile phone company office to win the game. His hysterical rant was interspersed with questions about his contract and accusations that I was having him followed. It went on for the best part of two hours. It was exhausting. It was also scary. After all, I had no idea what my houseguest was capable of. For all I knew, I had a Swedish axe murderer on my hands. Short of calling the police, I could see no way of getting rid of him. And calling the police had inherent complications at that time of night – especially with Sven in the drugged-up state that he was in.

At about 2.30 in the morning, I had had enough. I went to bed and told Sven that he should do the same 'for his own good'. I watched, relieved, as Sven headed across the patio and sauntered up the stairs to his room.

"What about the contract?" was the last comment I heard Sven say as he leaned over the upstairs balcony before entering his room.

I closed and bolted the back door of the main building and went to bed. I slept with my clothes on that night.

The following day I woke up at about 8 am – which was early for a Sunday. However, I was still wound up from the stress of the night before. I had hardly slept. I had spent the night wondering if the drugged-up Swede would come barreling into my part of the house and start questioning me threateningly about his contract. I felt safer now that it was daylight. I asked my guard Seila about Sven.

"Still sleeping, Sir," came the polite reply.

With that, I retired to the living room with a coffee. I was content to let my houseguest sleep off whatever he had taken the night before. I figured I would let him have a piece of my mind when he got up. I felt safer to do so in the daylight and with whatever drugs he had taken now worn off.

Nine o'clock rolled around - nothing. Then ten o'clock rolled around – nothing. And then, eleven o'clock – still nothing. It was at this point that I had had enough. I had things that I wanted to do. Sven was now ruining my one day off. I went up to his room.

"Hey, Sven!" I called through the door. "Time to get up. Let's go."

I was met with silence. There was no sound.

"Hey, come on! I need to get going," I tried again.

Again nothing.

I didn't call out a third time. Instead, I entered the room. The bed was unruffled and unslept, and there was no sign of my house guest anywhere. I even looked under the bed in case he had fallen off in the middle of the night. Nothing. There was absolutely no sign of him at all.

"Seila!"

Seila swore blind that he had not seen Sven leave. He said that he had locked the gate and that 'no one, absolutely no one' had asked him to open it in the middle of the night. Seila, who usually slept on a cot near the ten-foot-high gate and wall, was also completely baffled about how Sven could have 'escaped'. I phoned Jonno.

"Jonno? What the hell did you and Sven do last night?"

"Nothing, mate. We had a few beers and a Happy Herb's pizza," he replied.

"A Happy Herb's pizza!!! Are you out of your mind!?! What the hell were you thinking?"

"Mate...I did ask if he could handle it?" Jonno replied defensively.

"Well, he couldn't. He's disappeared," I said.

"Disappeared? No!?! Come to think of it, he was acting a bit strange. He jumped out of the car when I was going up Norodom Boulevard to another bar," Jonno mentioned casually.

"Jumped out of a moving car!?! And you didn't think to mention it to me?!? You know the guy's staying in my house," I responded incredulously. "What the hell's wrong with you?"

"Well, I thought it could wait until morning, mate," came the reply. "You looked stressed enough as it is."

"Well, we had better find him – otherwise, there will be hell to pay. The head office sent him," I said.

With that, Jonno and I toured guesthouses, hotels and hospitals in search of our missing sales manager. I called the company's 'mister fix it', who called the police, army and authorities. In doing so, he begged me not to mention speed, drugs, or Happy Herb's Pizza.

By five in the evening, there was still no news. I called Bradley, in his role as my country manager. He was on the golf course.

"Bradley, we've lost the sales candidate," I said sheepishly.

"What do you mean you've lost the sales candidate?" he asked incredulously.

I then told Bradley the whole story from beginning to end. He listened patiently and then laughed.

"Let's see if he shows up tonight," was his suggestion. "I'm in the middle of a round".

By nine the following day, I was sitting in Bradley's office at the mobile phone company with my head in my hands. I peered across at Bradley through tired eyes. It was the second night in a row that I hadn't slept.

"What the hell are we going to tell head office?" I asked Bradley.

"We can tell them that their candidate didn't cut it, and we're sending him back in a coffin," Bradley joked.

"Bradley, this is serious!"

"What do you want to tell them then?" Bradley asked. "Just tell them the truth – he went out, got drunk and drugged up and then disappeared."

"Yeah, but they will wonder what the hell is going on here and why we can't control our people," I replied.

"He's not one of our people," Bradley replied. "He's one of the head office's people. And he's a candidate and obviously can't handle the lifestyle. It's not for everybody, you know."

Just then, Bradley's office door flew open and in walked the Swede. He was still wearing the same ripped-up clothing that he was wearing two nights before.

"What about my contract?" were the first words that came out of his mouth.

"Get your bloody stuff and get out of my bleeding house," I shouted at him. It was an open-plan office, and I saw a hundred or so meek Cambodian faces apprehensively peering over their desktops. They were not used to seeing one *barang* lay into another *barang*. They smiled in embarrassment and then went about their business.

As I was to find out later, Sven had drunk several beers with Jonno and the other Aussies earlier in the evening. There, Sven had managed to hold his own. But then Jonno and Sven moved on to Happy Herb's Pizza. There, Jonno ordered a Happy Herb's Special. Sven ordered the same, and Jonno had asked Sven if he was sure he could handle it. Sven indicated he could, and they both tucked into their pizzas contentedly. To begin with, there was no effect.

Later, while Jonno was driving Sven to another bar, the pizza took effect, and he started flipping out.

"Where are you taking me?" he screamed.

"Just going to another bar, mate...." Jonno replied in typical Ocker Aussie fashion.

And then Sven jumped out of the car. Luckily it was a Toyota Rav 4, which was not very high off the ground. It was also moving at about 30 kilometres an hour – fast enough to cause some cuts, bruises, and possibly a fracture but not fast enough to do any real, lasting damage. As a result, Sven tore his clothes and grazed his hands and knees as he hit the ground. He then picked himself up and ran off. Jonno did a U-turn to go and find him, but by the time he got back to the spot where the Swede had ejected himself from the car, Sven was gone. Vanished.

Now entirely off his head from the Happy Herb's Special, Sven convinced himself he was in a reality TV show. He thought cameras were following him around town, capturing his every move. He also believed that to win the game, he had to get to the top of the four-storey mobile company headquarters – and that was where he headed.

Once there, he was stopped by the company's security guards. At first, they were bemused by this drunken *barang* – and then they were angry. He had become obstinate and was trying to fight his way in. They held him at bay. They then called the police to report a crazy foreigner trying to force his way into the company's head office. It was as the police arrived that Sven took off once again.

Just as Sven ran into the road, dodging *motos* and cars as he went, the 'good Samaritan' Australian nurse and her friends were passing by, only to peer out of their SUV to spot a dishevelled, drugged-up foreigner wandering around in the middle of the road. He looked disorientated and somewhat oblivious to the cars darting around him.

"We have to help him," the Australian nurse announced to her bemused fellow passengers. "He's going to get killed."

With that, the Australians stopped him, put him in their vehicle and searched him for a hotel or address. They found a scrunched-up scrap of paper bearing scrawled writing with my house address on it. They deposited him at my front gate and took off. However, the Australian nurse thought better of it and persuaded her fellow passengers to double back and see if the errant Swede would be OK. She appeared at my backdoor to satisfy herself that he would not be left to his own devices. She was confident that someone was there to look after him, so she divested herself of her responsibility. She then carried on with her own evening activities.

When I insisted that Sven go to bed, he appeared to do so. However, instead of going to sleep, he left his room, climbed over my ten-foot-high gate and wandered off down the road, where he came across a group of *moto-taxi* drivers. They tried to get his business, but he was having none of it and responded aggressively. They didn't like it, and the next thing, a scuffle broke out. He was then rescued by a passing *taxi-girl* (a Cambodian girl who prowled bars and nightclubs hoping to meet a foreigner for the evening). She then carted him off to the nearest guest house, where he spent the night and much of the next day cavorting with his newfound soulmate.

Late on Sunday, Sven came to his senses. He wondered what had happened to him. He didn't want to return to my house because he wasn't sure what had transpired there. He then opted for the only course of action he could think of. He went to the Swedish consul. He told the Swedish consul that he had been drugged. The Swedish consul believed him and brought him to our head office, determined to give our company a piece of his Swedish mind. That was until he heard the real story. Then, the penny dropped, and the consul realised that this was just another foreigner who had overdone it on the weed at Happy Herb's Pizza. Not wishing to become embroiled in such a time-wasting, trivial matter that was clearly the fault of the Swede himself, the consul took his leave.

Instead of leaving Cambodia - with his tail between his legs - Sven elected to stay to see if he had got the job.

"Hello, what about the contract?" was Sven's opening gambit on the phone a few days later.

"Look, Sven!" I replied incredulously. "Just get on a plane and get out of here. There is no job for you! Go!"

And he did.

YES, SIR, NO SIR, THREE BAGS FULL, SIR

WITH SVEN GONE, I turned my attention to other positions. As it happened, my first local hire was not for sales but engineering. He was a gentleman named Sothea, and he was a Chief Technical Officer who had been trained in Russia. In fact, he found me. When people heard about the new TV channel, the Phnom Penh employment grapevine went into overdrive. The country's media professionals began knocking on our door.

Sothea was one of the first. He came bounding into my office at the top of the mobile phone company's stairwell, where I had 'set up shop' while waiting for our offices to be ready. I conducted my first interview with a Khmer amongst the old filing cabinets, stacks of folders, and dusty documents I had inherited as part of my temporary office. Sothea didn't seem to mind the surroundings, however basic they were.

"I am honoured to meet you, Sir," Sothea said as he sat opposite me at the rickety wooden desk.

"No need to call me, Sir," I said, trying to put him at ease. "You can call me Glen."

"Yes, Sir," Sothea replied, fidgeting awkwardly in his plastic chair.

"It's Glen," I tried once again.

"OK, Sir."

And with that, I gave up. I resigned myself to the fact that the Cambodians would always be respectful to the point of subservience to a foreigner - unless, of course, they were some of the country's elite. Then they would often look down on all and sundry – apart from the Prime Minister. He alone seemed to command their respect. In fact, he commanded almost everyone's respect.

"So tell me about your experience?" I asked Sothea.

"Well, Sir...."

For the next ten minutes, I listened to how Sothea had effectively built Cambodia's broadcast industry single-handedly. He had been the engineer for the state broadcaster, the national radio station, and a whole host of other commercial broadcasters.

"But surely all these TV and radio stations you have set up compete with each other?"

"Yes, Sir. But I am the only qualified broadcast engineer in the country," Sothea replied shyly.

And with that, I hired Sothea on the spot. He was serious and qualified, and I hoped he would help me keep the errant Jonno on track and out of Happy Herb's Pizza long enough for him to build up our extensive transmission network. I also hoped that, with Sothea's impressive Russian training and qualifications, Jonno might actually learn something from him too. I just hoped Jonno would stay off the weed long enough to do so.

While finding a suitable local broadcast engineer proved much easier than I had ever imagined, finding other positions proved much more difficult. I placed ads in local newspapers and with a local recruitment firm to attract candidates. In return, I got back over 2000 CVs with all manner of applicants and applications. *Moto-taxi* drivers, tourist guides, farmers, market sellers and even former UNTAC trench diggers were there. I resigned myself to the fact that finding suitably qualified TV staff would be a real challenge.

Added to this challenge was that the head office demanded that I keep costs as low as possible. They were convinced that we would spend all of the company's money on a venture that they were sure was doomed to failure. On our weekly update calls, they insisted I keep the headcount low.

"Start from zero! Zero! Understood!?!" the head office would say. "Outsource as much as possible!"

It was hardly a ringing endorsement from my parent company for me or the start-up media venture they were now partners in - but I was getting used to this anyway.

"I'll never know why anyone would want to get into TV anyway. It's a dying medium!" was what I typically heard from the head office.

"I think it could be considered a strategic play," I would reply timidly.

"Hmmm! We are a mobile phone company, not a media company....this media thing is simply a means to an end. And it is a way to keep that local partner happy," Robert had said in Singapore.

Despite the lack of endorsement from head office, I set about building up my team bit by bit. And just like my first hire Sothea, everyone I interviewed called me 'Sir'. They also bowed and smiled as I approached or walked past – which made me feel embarrassed. After all, as a former journalist, I wasn't used to being treated with such reverence.

As journalists, officials were wary of us, and their bodyguards often shoved us around at every opportunity. In the news business – as in life - you had to have a pretty thick skin. In Cambodia, however, I had difficulty staying grounded with all the nodding, bowing, and smiling. I was definitely made to feel much more important than I actually was.

I cast my mind back to days gone by when I started out in journalism. On one of my first assignments with the BBC, I was firmly put in my place by the then morning show presenter.

I was at BBC Radio Suffolk at the time, when I was handed a story about a retiring milkman. BBC Radio Suffolk was based in Ipswich, and the beat was rural East Anglia.

The milkman was 'hanging up' his milk crate after 70 years on the job. Determined to give the would-be pensioner an auspicious radio send-off, I got fancy with the audio. I added some rattling milk bottles to the intro. We called it natural sound in the radio trade - or 'wild track' - and my initiative was pretty creative and imaginative - to my mind anyway. It even attracted the attention of the morning show celebrity presenter.

"Was that your piece this morning?" BBC Radio Suffolk's famous morning show host asked as he stopped by my desk after the piece had gone to air.

"Yes," I said, brimming with pride over my creative endeavours.

"We absolutely pissed ourselves laughing at that!" the famous presenter announced for the whole newsroom to hear. "You made it sound like the poor old codger had tripped over his bottles and killed himself! I don't know what he and his mates thought of it? He's probably a laughing stock down his local pub now."

It was a harsh induction to the news business, but it did teach me a valuable lesson. I learned that journalists rarely mince their words. They asked tough questions and made harsh statements – all in the name of truth. They appeared to be especially fierce in the broadcast sector, where everyone seemed to want to become famous.

As a hard-bitten, no-nonsense journalist used to the cut and thrust of the newsroom, I had to adjust my modus operandi somewhat and try to understand some of the culture thrust upon me.

Despite my best efforts to understand Cambodians and Cambodia, it was with a heavy heart that I opened up the email entitled - TV CAMERA - HOW CAN I DO? It went like this - in broken English -

Dear Sir,
I am so, so sorry. Please find it to forgive me. I had no
choice. Moto driver came driving to me but I could not
stop. He drive very fast and very crazy but how can I do?
If I hit him he hurt, may-be even die. How can I do? I am
so, so sorry. Please forgive me.
Sincerely,
Sreng
PS. TV Camera not working. It not turn on. I think it has
problem. Maybe we need to buy new one.

Upon further investigation, I discovered that Sreng had indeed driven my car into the river to avoid running over a wayward *moto* driver and his passenger. I also found out that the vehicle had been salvaged, but the TV camera inside had been completely destroyed.

After I had gotten over the initial shock and braced myself for the update call to the head office, I put the incident into perspective. I figured that in a 'good Buddhist society' such as Cambodia's, I could hardly expect a good Buddhist boy like Sreng to mow down his fellow countrymen just to save a material possession such as a car - or even a TV camera.

Another lesson I learned quickly is that Cambodians

laugh out of embarrassment and not just fun. I learned it while sacking our contingent of security guards at our newly built car park on the land that was to house our transmission tower.

"Sir, thief steal customer *moto*," Sreng said excitedly down the phone.

"It is six in the morning, Sreng. Why you call me? Call the police," I replied in the pidgin English I was now becoming accustomed to use to communicate with our staff. "And by the way, what customer? We don't have customer."

"Yes, Sir, but the security guard sells a ticket for parking customer *moto*."

"Sell ticket for what *moto*?"

"Security sells tickets for the student in a nearby school to park *moto*," Sreng explained, making it sound like it was standard practice.

"But it's our car park. We built it for us, not the students. They have no right to sell tickets – for us or for anyone or to anyone."

"Yes, but the customer's family is very angry."

"OK. Tell the family that we will investigate and get back to them."

"Will we buy a new *moto* for customer?"

"I don't know, Sreng! We will investigate."

We did investigate, and as it turned out, we were liable. By charging for tickets, the security guards had made us responsible for the well-being of the *motos* that were temporarily in their charge - and because they worked for us at the TV, we became liable by default too. I was fuming and let the security guards and everyone else know about it too. I shouted, kicked desks, and pounded fists on flimsy plastic tables that had been hastily arranged for my meeting in our car park near the tower with the security contingent.

"So you think you're clever, do you!?!" I bellowed, jabbing my finger at the twelve-strong security contingent now seated in the car park under the sweltering sun on plastic chairs. They squirmed as Sreng translated for me - in embarrassed tones.

"Do you!?!" I yelled. "So, do you?!?"

Blank faces stared back at me.

"How much did you make with this stunt!?!" I shouted. "Five dollars a month!?! Ten dollars a month!?!"

More blank stares.

"Well, you've just lost your salary! How do you feel about that!?! How much do you make!?! Fifty dollars a month?!? Well, you've lost it. Tell that to your wife...your girlfriend... your mother! Go on!"

With that, the security guards started to laugh.

"Oh, funny eh!?!" I shouted back at them.

More laughter.

"And now the police are involved too! Is that funny too!?! One of you will have to pay! One of you will go to jail!"

Even more laughter. It was at that point that Sreng sidled up to me. He approached cautiously, unsure of how I would react toward him too. He had never seen a *barang* quite this crazy before. He also needed to figure out how to educate me about the meaning of their laughing demeanour.

"Sir, Sir, they get it. They are not laughing at you, Sir. They're laughing because they are embarrassed, Sir. They very embarrassed. We Khmer very shy, Sir. You make them scared. You make me scared."

"Oh."

And with that, the twelve security guards signed their resignation letters. They were marched off towards the main gate by other security guards from a security firm that we had decided to employ in their stead. They fixed their eyes on the glistening tarmac as they made their way to the main gate. They refused to look up at me or anyone else as they walked. They had gotten the message loud and clear - so had our staff, which was growing to greater numbers and watching the whole spectacle unfold chaotically before them.

"Sir, Sir," Sreng called after me. "Some of the staff are scared. They say you are very angry and that they want to resign."

"What? No, no, no," I replied. "I was just doing that for effect. It's fine. I am not really that angry."

"OK, I'll tell them," Sreng replied. "But maybe you should tell them yourself. Maybe you should throw them dinner party to let them know you are happy?"

"What? Oh, all right," I replied. "You arrange it. I'll pay."

And so, having lost a 'customer's' motorbike, having got rid of our whole security contingent and having incurred additional wrath from head office for 'lack of controls in the workplace', I now had to buy everyone dinner. I was still scratching my head as I took my seat alongside my thirty-strong team as they tucked into noodle soup at a restaurant near our soon-to-be-finished tower.

SEM AND MISS BOPHA

It took us seven months to build the tower covering Phnom Penh. We had also paved and tarmacked the grounds in preparation for building the studio and office buildings. However, head office baulked just as we prepared to lay the foundations for the studio and office space. They began questioning the size of the buildings and the expenditure involved.

As it turned out, Oknha wanted a large studio, and the head office wanted to avoid paying for one. The head office favoured using existing office space.

I cast my mind back to my meeting with Yann in Singapore.

"By the way, how big do we need to build the studio?" Yann had asked.

"About as big as this room," I replied naively.

"Good," Yann had replied.

I decided not to inform Oknha about that particular

conversation. I hoped they wouldn't use the 'TV man's' comment to justify their recalcitrance.

Nevertheless, Oknha argued that we would need to stage singing contests, concerts, and broadcast debates and forums to attract and keep an audience. He also advocated creating content for the future. At the same time, the head office argued that media was not the company's core business. The head office dug in and absolutely refused to spend money on something that they thought was unnecessary and superfluous.

Oknha, on the other hand, played the prime ministerial card saying that the PM expected a certain level of investment for those doing business in Cambodia. At that particular point in the company's Cambodian evolution, the company was falling well short of the amount expected. A standoff between the two joint venture partners followed, bringing our operation to a standing stop.

"Just build it anyway!" Oknha ordered irritably.

"Where is the money coming from?" I asked respectfully. "We are not making a profit yet."

"Hmmm, hmmm, hmmm," Oknha replied, indicating that he was at a loss for words and had no answers.

By the time our operation had come to a standstill, I had hired about thirty staff who were already undergoing training on television production and presentation, scheduling and sales. We were also starting to pre-sell advertising space and sponsored programs. At first, I was at a loss to explain the delay, but then I became creative with my excuses.

"We are discussing a major deal with overseas media

companies that could change the face of Cambodian broadcasting," was one excuse I used.

"We are buying the latest state-of-the-art technology from overseas, and there is a major backlog in orders," I said, unfairly passing the blame on to the equipment suppliers.

Apart from waiting, I spent more time at home with little else to do. When I got bored there, I was out and about socialising in the numerous hole-in-the-wall bars that made up Phnom Penh's after-work leisure scene.

Luckily, the company believed in treating its management with a semblance of civility. As such, they provided a generous housing allowance that enabled me to find comfortable living quarters. Realising, as I did, that Phnom Penh in 2002 was still considered a 'hardship posting', I took my time to find a comfortable house to live in. The place I found was Lucky Villa, which was just down the road from the American Embassy and SOS Clinic.

Lucky Villa was effectively a compound hidden by ten feet high walls and a massive steel gate. From the outside, it looked like a fortress. However, once inside the grounds, the main building and its quaint guesthouse were practical, comfortable and somewhat ornate. A grey-brown gravel drive led up to the main house with lush sprinkled lawns on either side framed by flower beds with various coloured blossoms. Off to the side near the massive stone walls was a row of frangipani trees intermingled with papaya and mango trees. A covered patio with a large dining table and assorted rattan lounge chairs was at the back of the house. There, I ate my meals and spent most of my time socialising with friends and holding informal meetings with staff.

I also had my own security guard and a maid called Sem.

Sem had a broad, weather-beaten face, dark wavy hair that reached the nape of her neck and a severe, no-nonsense, get-things-done outlook on life that helped her to overcome any challenge that the world – and Cambodia in particular – had thrown at her.

Sem had a solid build, unlike other Cambodian ladies, who were often petite. To her fellow countrymen – and women – she was considered stout. And I must admit I often watched in wonder as she arrived for work on a two feet high Honda Charly scooter with her haunches spilling out over the sides and her whole upper body dwarfing the scooter's minuscule frame. I found it quite comical to watch her mount her little Honda Charly and even funnier to watch her spur the little machine into action and wobble down the boulevard at 15 kilometres an hour.

Although her appearance on the scooter might have been comical, her background certainly wasn't. Sem had seen it all. Not only had she survived the Khmer Rouge, being forced to wed a man she didn't know, but she had also brought up her daughter during the early 90s when the Khmer Rouge were still in evidence, and fighting had broken out on the streets of Phnom Penh between Prime Minister Hun Sen and his then co-Prime Minister Prince Norodom Ranariddh. It was Prime Minister Hun Sen who had won that round - and had continued to win ever since. And to Sem's mind, he was the only one who could bring peace to this war-torn country. That fact made her an ardent supporter of the ruling CPP and Prime Minister Hun Sen himself.

"With Samdech, we have no war," Sem would say with respect and admiration, using the Prime Minister's honorific title. "I want CPP. I don't want war. Sem have enough war."

Many others shared Sem's sentiments. They made up a group of men and women who were forty- and fifty-something and who had survived the Khmer Rouge and witnessed the fighting that had followed. Some persevered and survived, while others perished. Those who survived just wanted peace at any cost and didn't really care for the politics of the matter. They just wanted to go about their lives without fearing for their own safety or that of their children. Having lost everything before, they were content with what they had now – regardless of how little that was. For those who survived, the families and the children that they now had at their side were everything. Nothing else mattered as long as they could live peacefully with their husbands, wives, and children.

After the violence had dissipated and things had settled down in the late 90s, Sem was one of the lucky ones. At a time when there were no jobs to speak of, and the desperation of war had been replaced by the anguish of everyday survival, Sem said that she had found a job at the French Embassy in Phnom Penh. They had apparently taught her how to cook, clean, and keep house there. So when she eventually happened on my doorstep at Lucky Villa in downtown Phnom Penh in 2002, she appeared to be an accomplished cook and housekeeper. She was also highly professional in attitude and demeanour. She would arrive at seven on the dot every morning, often with hot croissants and a baguette in her basket, which she would serve alongside a steaming cup of hot coffee. Once served, she would disappear into the house and start polishing the bits and pieces I had inherited from the house's previous tenants and the owner. And then, after that, she would start on the laundry.

Sem threw herself into her work and tackled every task with gusto, determination and pride. No job was ever beneath her, no matter how menial. I often wondered if her work ethic and overall attitude were a product of her time suffering under the Khmer Rouge or just a way to keep her mind occupied and forget her hurtful past. However, she never spoke about those times, so I doubted I would ever know.

"With Samdech, we have no war," was all she would say on the matter.

While Sem was conscientious, thoughtful and diligent, her husband was the exact opposite. She had inherited him during the Khmer Rouge when she was forced to marry and had stuck with him through thick and thin. However, while Sem accepted her own deprived lot in life, her husband hadn't, and he turned to drinking. Sem's husband preferred to spend most of his time drinking in local beer gardens and massage parlours, cavorting with eighteen-year-old beer girls, hostesses and waitresses. He came home when he wanted to and in whatever state he saw fit without any consideration for the welfare of Sem or their daughter Sophea.

When Sem berated him for his irresponsible behaviour, as she often did, Sem's husband would resort to violence, lashing out with his fists and anything else he could get his hands on. I learned about it after she worked for me for about six weeks.

One night I was sitting at home when I received a tearful phone call late at night.

"He no good!" Sem wailed down the phone. "Please help me?"

Once I understood what was going on – which was no mean task considering Sem's incoherent state, I told her to come and stay with me in my guest rooms at the back of the house. And so she did. Sem brought with her plastic bags full of clothes and belongings - and her twenty-something daughter. And so after a little over a month and a half in my employ, Sem was no longer just a maid - she was now a live-in maid too. It had not been part of the initial agreement, but plans change - and rules are made to be broken. Not only was she my live-in maid, but she became my middle-aged 24-hour concierge and master chef too. Her daughter Sophea became her understudy and sous chef. I was waited on hand and foot for a time by a fifty-something lady and her twenty-something daughter. It was good while it lasted.

Unbeknown to me, Sem then met someone new, having left her drunken spouse. She did so in the inordinate hope of improving her lot - and that of her daughter Sophea. Finding a good man became her focus. She saw it as a means to an end - a way to improve her and her daughter's lot in life. After all, they had both already suffered enough.

After a few months, Sem met a Cambodian-American man. He had fled the country during the Khmer Rouge and went to Long Beach in California. How the Cambodian-American man met Sem was anyone's guess and a complete mystery to me too. They had both known each other before the days of the Khmer Rouge. He was one of the lucky ones who had been able to flee to the United States, obtain a green card and settle down. Sem had been forced to endure everything that Cambodia's recent history had thrown at her – and, with her errant 'inherited Khmer Rouge' spouse, even more.

The Cambodian-American man proposed, and Sem readily accepted. After all, her fiance had decent prospects in the West. And even though the marriage meant leaving her troubled homeland - and her daughter - behind, Sem figured that it was a price worth paying to have a better life. Sem knew, in her heart of hearts, that it would be best for her daughter too. She consoled herself in knowing that Sophea would join her in the United States one day. So, it was with measured joy that Sem hastily arranged a wedding ceremony for herself and her Cambodian-American groom.

It was a simple ceremony at a local hotel, and I was the guest of honour. It seemed that my presence gave an air of legitimacy to the whole proceedings, which I couldn't help feeling was being staged to appease a watchful and increasingly suspicious department of United States Immigration.

I arrived at about lunchtime and took my place on a mat on the floor. Rice was doled out, as were soft drinks. There were then plenty of happy snaps - with me in them.

I had visions of pictures of my good self being used as evidence in Sem's application for a green card.

"See? *Barang* man come to our wedding," I pictured her pleading at the US Embassy just down the road from me.

However she achieved it, I was happy that Sem would finally get a new life. It took precedence over my domestic bliss, which I was sure would now take a turn for the worse. After all, I had been living the life of Riley for some months. But, I should have known better. Being as conscientious as she was, Sem had already conjured up a plan.

"Don't worry, Sir, my daughter very good cook. She look after you," Sem said as she wheeled her United States-bound luggage to the waiting Toyota Camry. "I teach her much."

"But she very young...." I started to be mindful that I would now have a twenty-something maid living alone in my house. I wondered what my neighbours would think - let alone what head office would say when they found out, which I was sure they would.

"No problem, Sir. She good girl," Sem called out through the open window as the Toyota Camry slid past me down the drive on her way to the airport.

And so it was that the domestic bliss I had become so used to changed overnight. And while Sem might have given her daughter some lessons on cooking and housekeeping, Sophea did not have the same knack for either that her mother had. As a result, within a week of Sem leaving, I was floored by a stomach bug so nasty that it rendered me incapable of leaving the house or, at times, even the toilet.

Once I had finally recovered after three days of churning stomachs and bowels, I awoke to find that Sophea had written me a note. It read as follows -

Sir, I so sorry, Sir. I not want to make sick you. I not want cook you. My mother tell me have to have job and that you good man and you no mind new cook. But I cannot. So I go now.

No sooner had I finished the handwritten scrawl when the phone rang, and it was Sem. She apologised profusely for her daughter's culinary faux pas.

"She think bacon is the same ham," Sem explained. "I teach her to cook bacon, but she not understand."

It was morning in Cambodia and evening in the United States. Sem then informed me that she was in Las Vegas, where she had found a job as a croupier in a casino. She said she was just starting her shift but had to call me to tell me that her sister would now come and cook for me.

"You no worry!" Sem bellowed down the phone. "My sister very good lady. She look after you good! She know difference ham and bacon. She good."

Unused to making international calls, Sem seemed to think that the further you were away from the person you were calling, the louder you had to speak. Seeing as Las Vegas was almost 10,000 miles away, she was shouting very loudly. I had to hold the phone a good six inches from my ear just to decipher her words and protect my eardrums. I was also worried that I would disturb my neighbours, who would no doubt be able to hear a heavily accented English-speaking Khmer woman shouting down the phone at me - even through the thin metal fence that separated our adjoining patios and homes. I was worried that they might think I had knocked up Sem's daughter and that I was being read the long-distance riot act in broken English.

"Sem, please don't worry. It will be fine," I reassured her. "How's your husband?"

"He in Califonia. I, Las Vegas," and then she returned to the matter at hand. "My sister, she come now."

Within a minute or so I heard a phone ringing nearby and then another lady screeching down the phone in Khmer. However, this one was in my garden - not Las Vegas. The noise was followed by the appearance of a solid-looking, weather-beaten Khmer lady being escorted up the drive by my guard Seila. She reminded me somewhat of Sem.

"Sir, lady say she have appointment," Seila explained as she accompanied the Sem-lookalike to me.

"Yes, I know her. Thanks, Seila," I replied.

"My name Bopha," the lady said as she handed over a reference from the French Embassy and a certificate of English.

"I can speaking English very good," Miss Bopha informed me proudly.

"Yes, I can tell," I smiled back.

She handed me a reference. The paper was smudged. and it looked remarkably like the reference Sem had handed me over six months ago.

"I cook same same sister," Miss Bopha announced.

"Yes, I'm sure you do," I replied.

As it turned out, Miss Bopha was an excellent cook as well as a stickler for detail. She passed my tests with flying colours - and more.

Not only did Miss Bopha add a touch of class to my daily dining rituals, but she also seemed to be genuinely concerned for my dietary welfare. She would stand over me and watch to make sure that I ate all the papaya she served up for dessert and only allow me to have two cups of coffee daily.

"Papaya good for skin," she would say. "Coffee not good for sleep."

Within a few weeks, I had all but forgotten Sem and her daughter Sophea. There seemed to be little doubt that I was in very safe hands with Miss Bopha - whether or not she really was Sem's sister.

ON THE TOWN

JUST LIKE MANY RELATIONSHIPS, Miss Bopha and I had something of a honeymoon period. It was time spent dancing around each other. We were like boxers sizing one another up in the ring. She weighed me up just as I weighed her up. And although I could not fault her for her efficiency and commitment to housework, I was concerned that she was overstepping her housekeeping bounds.

Right from the start, her maternal instincts kicked in, and she started treating me as if I was some irresponsible teenager. She seemed to think it was her responsibility to straighten me out and get - what she thought was - my wayward persona back on the straight and narrow. However, I was happy with the way things were. Besides, her attitude was not in keeping with how I saw myself - as the 40-year-old master of the house.

Miss Bopha disapproved of me drinking or coming home late. In her opinion, Phnom Penh after dark was a dangerous place to be. She seemed to lose sight of the fact that I spent all my working days surrounded by Khmers who, although they were good friends, did not go in for the kind of banter and wind-ups that I was nominally used to in England and elsewhere. For that, I would join the Aussies and Brits for early after-work drinks.

I was starting to feel like I was back at boarding school in Sussex and that the worst of the matrons had been assigned to whip me into shape. Yet, despite her no-nonsense matronly manner, I couldn't fault her for her work ethic or her honesty. On one occasion, when I came home somewhat the worse for wear from drink, I left three hundred dollars on the coffee table in the living room. When I woke up, it was gone. However, even though I had been drunk and fuzzy-headed, I knew I hadn't spent it. I began to fear the worst. I began to think Miss Bopha had pocketed my money, thinking I would be too hungover to notice. I didn't relish the inevitable confrontation I knew the situation would incur. After all, I was still smarting from my run-in with our laughing studio security guards.

Having made up my mind to bring up the subject of the missing money, I trundled out onto the patio at eight o'clock in the morning. I sat down at my usual spot at the breakfast table. I was wondering how I would let Miss Bopha go when I felt a heavy clout to the back of my head.

"Hey, Bopha!" I protested, dropping my usual respectful Miss in the process. "What the hell's that for?"

"You crazy or what?" Miss Bopha started at me as she threw three one-hundred-dollar bills on the table before me. "Why you no care your money. You no like money, you give Miss Bopha. Miss Bopha happy take your money! Miss Bopha need money!"

Seeing as Miss Bopha only earned one hundred dollars a month, an acceptable wage in 2002 in Cambodia, the sight of three hundred dollars sitting on the table must have been a temptation indeed.

However, as she had demonstrated with her actions, she was hard-working and honest. And I felt pangs of guilt for having misjudged her. I immediately rid myself of any notion of dismissing her and gave her a fifty-dollar monthly raise instead. She was so happy that she bowed and said *okun* in thanks more than twenty times until I told her to stop because she was embarrassing me.

"And by the way...if I want to go out drinking, I'll go out drinking!" was my parting shot after I had given her the raise. Satisfied that I had done the right thing, I reached for an iced glass of water to take my aspirin to help cure my hangover – a product from the night before - and hopefully ease my guilty conscience somewhat in the process.

"You, crazy man," Miss Bopha muttered, signalling that the pay increase would not mean she would let go of her responsibilities as defacto matron. "Crazy *barang*! Never learn."

I smiled as I watched her disappear into the kitchen to make me my morning coffee.

Working as we did, with the daily frustrations that we generally faced, going out for a beer became an essential part of my stress-busting routine. With this in mind, I joined the other expats from the mobile phone company's head office to assemble for after-work drinks at a bar in the town centre.

My after-work bar of choice was a sports bar called The Gym. It was owned by an Australian called Rory, who excelled in making pub grub. Cottage and shepherd's pies and chilli con carne were his fortes.

"Where is Rory?" I asked one day upon walking in. I usually had a beer with him before the others from the mobile phone company arrived.

"He's in the chicken," the barmaid replied.

Her response stopped me in my tracks.

"Chicken?"

"Yes, he is in the chicken."

"I don't see a chicken," I said.

"He's in the chicken," the barmaid replied again, rolling her eyes.

This time she pointed over my shoulder to the kitchen.

"There," she said emphatically. "In the chicken."

"Ah ha," I replied, finally cottoning on to her linguistic faux pas. "In the kitchen! Righto!"

Her mistake was familiar enough. In everyday speech, Cambodians regularly mixed up the word 'chicken' with the word 'kitchen'. They did the same with 'glass' and 'mirror'.

Having established that Rory was in the kitchen, I took a place at the bar where most clientele gathered, clutching their Angkor beers and swapping anecdotes that summed up their working day or week. There was usually no shortage of humour or banter. There was also often no shortage of beers or pretty local girls working as bar staff.

While The Gym was the place to start the evening, those who wanted to go on would end up at The Cathouse or

Frontier, depending on how late one wanted to be – and the kind of company one wanted to keep.

The Cathouse was a Phnom Penh mainstay. As a watering hole, it was set up in the days of UNTAC to cater to the thousands of foreigners drafted in to oversee the country's attempted transition to normalcy after its demise at the hands of the Khmer Rouge. As such, some of the previous clientele had been soldiers serving with the United Nations force. As a result, the previous owner had worryingly found it necessary to place a prominent sign at the entrance declaring NO FIRE-ARMS ALLOWED (Please leave your weapons at the door). Though this might have appeared menacing, especially to those not in the know, it was merely a throwback to days gone by and was now more iconic than realistic. At the turn of the millennium in Cambodia, there were very few foreign servicemen in the country - and those living there no longer bore sidearms because the security situation had improved immensely. There was simply no longer any need. Nevertheless, the plaque remained. It added an air of nostalgic mystery to The Cathouse.

As entertainment establishments went, The Cathouse was nothing special from the outside. In fact, there was nothing to set The Cathouse apart from any other building in the street. It was located a few blocks from the city's Central Market and occupied the lower floor of a Cambodian shophouse. It had an understated-looking entrance with a light grey door set into a whitewashed façade. There was little signage and branding; you could have driven past it quite easily if you didn't know where it was. If anything, the bar had a 'speakeasy' feel, adding to the 'off-limits' mystique.

Once inside, the bar began to take on an opium den-type feel. Punters huddled at the establishment's circular bar, where wafts of white smoke circled around the red lanterns that dangled from the ceiling. However, it was cigarette smoke, not opium, and a 60s rock song provided an atmospheric backing track to the muffled – almost whispered – conversations that were taking place at the bar.

While The Cathouse was good for pool and catching up on some local gossip, Street 51, where Frontier, Cupid, and a few other bars were, was much more raucous. It was a ragged, rundown back street with potholes and broken pavements, which only came alive around eleven at night. Those who liked to partake of a 'Happy Herb's Special without the pizza' - often frequented it.

As it happened, Frontier used to be a backpacker hangout with the dubious claim to fame of serving free joints to anyone who entered. The joints were placed in glass bowls near the door and were there for the taking by adventurous Western travellers – and, of course, local expats. Before I got to Phnom Penh, partygoers used to help themselves to the free joints. They stopped the practice after the turn of the millennium, so now disco and house music reverberated loudly around the various rooms that made up the establishment.

When I had had my fill of pulsating dance music, I moved to one of the quieter bars down the strip, like Cupid Bar.

What Cupid Bar lacked in house music and gyrating revellers, it made up for in interesting characters. There were war veterans, NGOs, English teachers and the odd mercenary who sat taking their tipples at the bar. All of them laughed and joked with the attractive hosts. Almost all of them stayed there until the early hours of the morning.

One night I walked into the Cupid Bar to find a fellow Brit sitting at the bar with his Cambodian girlfriend. We talked, and it turned out that he was an ex-United States Marine who had also served as a mercenary in Bosnia.

"A Brit serving with the Yanks? How did that happen?"

"Long story," he replied, not wishing to be drawn on the subject.

However, he was less reticent about his mercenary endeavours in the former Yugoslavia. As it turned out, he had been fighting in Bosnia while I was in Sarajevo, covering the war as a journalist. We compared notes and started good-naturedly throwing Bosnian swearwords at one another. It was my way of testing those who had said they had been there. By all accounts, this particular ex-mercenary had definitely served time there, judging by the quality and quantity of the swear words he knew. Not only could he swear like a trooper, he could also swear like a Bosnian trooper.

While trading Bosnian insults and anecdotes, my newfound friend appeared to get deadly serious. I thought I had upset him and was preparing to duck or make a run for it.

"I have skills that others don't. You mark my words,". At first, I thought he was talking about his penchant for hurting and killing people. Either that or, indeed, he was even making a veiled threat. And then he smiled, "Hey, you watch this!"

The mercenary then smashed a glass on the counter and ground the glass up in a cloth. He then popped the shards and splinters into his mouth. He chewed the glass cud for a full minute and then swallowed, smiling.

"All gone," he said proudly.

"What the hell!" I exclaimed. "How did you do that?"

"Easy," he replied. "Just make sure you grind the glass up good and proper. It's perfectly safe. I've been doing it for years."

It wasn't quite as safe as my new mercenary friend had made out. I later heard that he died some months after. I can't say that it surprised me. I remember thinking then that a man who considers eating glass an amusing party trick would not have much shelf-life. And I made sure that I didn't tell Miss Bopha about my newfound friend. She already considered night-time Phnom Penh dangerous, with or without glass-chewing mercenaries.

Although she never found out about the mercenary, she found out about some other nocturnal happenings. One, in particular, stood out – and this time, it involved the police. Though I was effectively an innocent bystander.

The whole episode took place on a Saturday night. At the time, I sat inside the Cupid Bar, talking to fellow patrons. It was about midnight, and Street 51's nightlife scene was in full swing, building to a post-midnight crescendo. Usually, at that time, there was the pulsating throb of dance music emanating from the bars that lined the strip. The throbbing beat of dance music mingled with the high-pitched hoots and hollers of inebriated backpackers as they tumbled in and out of Frontier and other bars along the strip.

However, at about one in the morning, there came the sound of another kind of noise. It was the sound of metal shearing metal and the bump and clatter of collision and chaos. The noise was accompanied by the shocked yelps and screams of those on the street outside.

Startled by the unfamiliar din, I looked up and down the street. To my horror, I peered out to see that the cars that had been neatly parked in a line along the street up to a few moments ago were now strewn across the road haphazardly. Where there had been order, there was now chaos. The cars and *motos* were now completely askance. It was as if a giant tornado had come through the area and picked up all of the cars, SUVs and *motos*, then dumped them willy-nilly in the middle of the road. It was a chaotic scene made even more so by the thirty-strong revellers now standing in the middle of the thoroughfare gossiping in drunken animation. They feigned shock and horror but secretly relished that they had become part of a potentially dangerous event. If nothing else, it would give them something to tell their friends back home – another leaf out of the brief but adventurous backpacking chapter of their life.

I approached a group of sun-tanned, tank-topped foreigners and asked what was happening.

"It was that guy over there," the tourist replied, pointing up the street towards a bar which occupied pride of place on the corner of the Street 51 strip. "He came hurtling down here, bouncing off all these cars. He did a load of damage. Luckily, no one was hurt. He must be plastered."

"Yes, very lucky," I replied. I was relieved that my car was still parked at the end of the street on the corner where I had left it some hours before. It looked like it had escaped unscathed. Not wishing to become embroiled in what I was sure would become complicated officialdom, I paid my Cupid Bar bill and ambled toward my car to head home. I looked to see if there was anyone I knew among the revellers. There wasn't. It was already late, and I was sure I would be woken by the clunk and clatter of Miss Bopha's vacuum cleaner at my door the following day.

As I strolled up the street away from the onlookers, I noticed my car was different from how I had left it. It was now in a strange position up against a skinny tree. On closer inspection, I noticed that the car had been moved about a foot from where I had initially parked it. And as I gingerly sidled up to the vehicle, I noticed that the driver's door was now wedged up against the tree I had spotted earlier.

As I surveyed the scene before me, I could only guess that the perpetrator of this accident had bounced off every car in the street before hitting mine. Then after he had hit my car, he had bounced off again, careering across the road only to end up parked on the pavement outside the bar at the corner of the street. As I looked across at the offending vehicle – a Land Cruiser – I could also see what looked like the offending driver sitting on the pavement, resting his head in his hands in shocked disbelief at the havoc he had managed to wreak.

"Are you all right?" I asked.

"Mate, she cut my brakes," the man announced with slurred speech.

"Yes, but are you all right?" I repeated.

"I'm fine, mate. But that 'sheila' cut my brakes! I broke up with her last week. She's a Khmer girl."

"OK, let's deal with that later," I replied. "You hit my car pretty hard. You wrapped it around a tree. It's probably the only tree in the street, and you found it. Now I can't drive home."

"Sorry, mate. It was that 'sheila'," the man replied.

I studied him for a minute and concluded that his repetitive use of the Aussie slang 'sheila' identified him as an Aussie.

"Well, you're going to have to explain that to this lot," I replied, gesturing towards a police pickup truck that had just appeared on the street. A police unit sat stoically in the back as they surveyed the scene and the crowd forming. They waited for orders to dismount. And when they came, the surly-faced guards leapt out and took control of the street, blocking the road and gathering up the onlookers as they moved into position.

"Please, you no move!" the senior policeman told me. "We investigate."

"I'm not involved," I replied. "That is my car there. I got hit."

"We keep for proof," the policeman replied.

I groaned. The last thing I wanted was to be embroiled in a police investigation in the middle of the night. I then watched as a flatbed truck appeared on the street and started carting damaged vehicles away one by one. Because my car was at the end of the street, mine was the last to go. By this time, it was 5.30 am, and the sky was starting to lighten.

"Please, drive your car to the police station," the commanding officer instructed. "Truck busy with other cars."

"But I have been drinking," I responded.

"No problem. You follow the police car," he said with a straight face.

And with that, I clambered into my car through the passenger door, slid over the gear stick and inserted myself into the driver's side. I did as I was instructed by Cambodia's police and drove myself over the limit to the police station.

"Only in Cambodia!" I said aloud to myself. "Only in Cambodia!"

When I arrived home, it was six thirty in the morning, and the sun had already risen. The morning had the makings of a blisteringly hot Cambodian day ahead of it - and it would be one that I was determined to spend sleeping off the adventures of the night before. A police vehicle dropped me at Lucky Villa.

"You crazy man!" Miss Bopha called out as I stepped through the gate into the safety of my own home. "What you do now? Why you bring problem with police?"

"Miss Bopha, not now, please," I pleaded hoarsely as I prepare for my matronly housekeeper to start in on me. "It's been a long night. Let me have a glass of water."

Miss Bopha stopped, looked at me intently and then backed off. She could tell I was in no mood for an argument. I went into the house and went to bed. It was almost seven in the morning at that time.

Later the same day, when I had woken, I told Miss Bopha about the night's events. She listened stoically and then got on her *moto* and drove off. At first, I thought she had had enough and had decided to leave my employ, finally fed up with the crazy *barang's* ways. I resigned myself to the fact that I would now have to find yet another housekeeper.

I then heard the gate swing open. Miss Bopha appeared on her Honda Charly *moto* in the drive. She wore a determined look on her face and carried a bundle under her arm.

"This is Showkie," Miss Bopha announced as a charcoal black snout appeared beneath a cloth. "You need to take care. Your new friend. Now you no go out so much at night. You have responsibility. You have dog."

Showkie looked at me, and I looked at him. He probably had no inkling as to the gravity of his newfound responsibility.

And that was that. Miss Bopha stayed, and I became the proud owner of a Cambodian street dog named Showkie.

MARRY ME, MR. GLEN

I have only been proposed to once in my life, and it happened in a bar called Freestyle on a tree-lined boulevard in the heart of Phnom Penh.

Freestyle was located just off Norodom Boulevard. It occupied the bottom section of a Chinese shophouse. It had a massive floor-to-ceiling shutter that was almost always up and open to the street, with raucous music and banter emanating from there after dark.

It was a favourite haunt for many Australian and New Zealand expats so there was usually no shortage of humour or banter. There was also usually no shortage of beers or pretty local girls working as bar staff.

As the evening wore on, the noise levels would rise, and the standards of decorum would fall. The session would usually culminate in someone brushing up against the ship's bell strategically placed near the pretty Khmer girl working as a cashier near the till. Sonorous peels would ring out when one hapless customer or another brushed up against the bell. The bar momentarily stopped as whoops and cheers also rang out across the room. Sounding the bell – inadvertently or not – meant buying the whole house a drink. While drinking at Freestyle, I must have spent a few thousand dollars buying the house a drink over the years and wasn't alone. However, I still blame the attractiveness of the cashiers, whose sole roles in life were counting money and distracting paying customers with their looks and flirtatious manner.

On one particular occasion, I had spent an after-work hour catching up on expat happenings with the mobile phone crew and opted to linger. I had avoided the ship's bell on this occasion but wanted to delay going home.

I was finishing off my last beer when Amy sidled up to me. She worked in the bar and was in her twenties. She was also extremely pretty. She was of average height, standing at 5 feet tall or so with slender legs and a slim, shapely torso. Her long dark blue-black hair was impeccably straight and fell glistening to the middle of her back, where it clung delicately to her white sleeveless top. She had walnut-coloured skin with high cheekbones and an oval-shaped face that broke easily into a radiantly perfect smile. And above all, she had a sense of humour. She could make a joke and take one too.

"Marry me, Mr. Glen?" she pleaded.

I spat out some of my beer.

"I have a French girlfriend," I countered. "She is in the UK."

And it was true. I still did have my French girlfriend. We had been together for years. She had even made the trip out to Phnom Penh. She was considering moving out permanently – if her own work commitments allowed.

As for Amy, she had just been jilted by a New Zealand boyfriend. His name was Keith. And while he had enjoyed Amy's friendship, she had been looking for more. He had told her he wasn't in the market for a Khmer wife earlier that night. Amy had put a brave face on it but was determined to replace Keith with another – and I looked available. I was also alone - or so she thought because she had never seen me with another woman.

In 2003 Cambodia, an expat husband was considered a valuable commodity for some Khmer girls. Oknha had even called such liaisons part of the unofficial poverty reduction program because they helped lift the female population segment. Whether such a statement was politically correct was a matter of opinion, but the practice was based on fact. I knew of a few such couples myself.

In fact, when I first arrived in Phnom Penh, I learned of an Irish man who was 'claimed' by a young, pretty Khmer girl. She was an employee of the mobile phone company, so she was self-sufficient. However, this did not stop her from 'claiming' her man. She started going out with the expat manager. And when she had got him, she wasn't about to let go.

"When I came home one night, I found that she had moved her fridge and all her worldly possessions in," the manager had said. "When I questioned her about her actions and said it was a bit soon in the relationship, she merely shrugged and said there was no point in paying two rents. She is still with me today."

As it happened, that particular couple got married and

had three children. However, they did end up divorcing years later, so the marriage may not have been based on firm enough foundations.

One of the reasons why some of the Khmer women might have favoured expat husbands might well have been that arranged marriages were still a feature of Khmer society. It was not uncommon for families to look for a spouse for their offspring. This was particularly the case with girls. There were also incidents of girls trying to commit suicide or run away because their parents had chosen the wrong mate for them. So, as Amy sat before me, stating the case for us getting married, I couldn't help wondering if her underlying motive was trying to avoid an arranged marriage.

"I cook very good," Amy continued. "I speak goodly English. I look after you very, very goodly too."

"Amy, you are very beautiful, but I do not want to get married just yet," I replied as I finished my beer. "I have a French girlfriend."

"Oh," came the reply. "Buy me a drink, Mr .Glen?"

And that I did. I figured it would help her drown her sorrows.

As it happened, Amy married a few weeks later to a French man. He was a hotelier and a chef, and they embarked on a relationship where they lived together and worked together. They also had two children. It seemed to work, and they both appeared happy.

While Amy achieved her objective, millions of others didn't. They would vicariously experience their romance by watching our Thai dramas or Khmer movies. The storylines for both consisted primarily of love triangles. Usually, a rich boy or girl would meet a poor boy or girl and fall in love. However, the parents usually had other plans and would want the boy or girl to meet a 'more suitable' rich mate. The result was a lot of unhappiness, skulking around, and, of course, drama. It was watchable entertainment because the Khmers could relate to such goings-on.

In reality, Khmer society was quite conservative. It wasn't uncommon for courting couples to bring a chaperone on a first date, and sex before marriage was frowned upon. There was also little knowledge about birth control and the dangers of promiscuity. Sometimes it fell to the NGOs to take the lead in teaching youngsters about sex.

On TV we would have to be careful, I was told by Oknha. We would be unable to show dating programs and beauty contests involving Khmer women wearing swimsuits were also off-limits. I had even heard talk that the Prime Minister's wife, Bun Rany, was a staunch advocate of respecting Cambodian females. It was her mandate that beauty contests and risqué pageants be banned.

I had even heard that one TV station had gotten in trouble for allowing a singer to appear with a backless top.

"The Prime Minister called the owner and shouted at him," our head of news, Mr. Som, told me. "The owner said that while he was being yelled at by the Prime Minister himself, he could also hear the Prime Minister's wife shouting in the background. The concert was stopped mid-show. There was no explanation. It just disappeared."

As for ourselves, I received a call from Oknha about our plans to air Benny Hill. I was sitting in Freestyle bar one night when the phone rang.

"Are we going to be OK?" Oknha asked. "The general says that the Prime Minister might not approve."

The general to whom Oknha referred had just visited our hi-tech broadcasting facility and viewed a few program clips. One of the clips he viewed was Benny Hill.

"We will be fine, Oknha. Trust me," I replied. "Benny Hill is foreign. It doesn't disrespect Khmer culture."

I had had a few beers by the time this particular call had come in, but I did think that we would be fine. And if we weren't, the controversy would help the ratings. Besides, I wanted to return to my beer and the Aussie banter.

In addition to being conservative, the older generation of Khmers was also strict with their children – and this also went all the way to the top. Every Valentine's Day, the Prime Minister would remind Cambodia's young people not to get 'carried away'. Sex before marriage was entirely out of the question. We had to be careful about showing it on TV.

We also had to blur guns – which created a challenge in airing Hong Kong dramas where triads and gangsters regularly pulled guns on one another and had multiple shoot-outs. Smoking could be shown – for the time being, anyway and there was no watershed for alcohol back then either. All in all, the whole sector was fairly unregulated.

The one thing we really had to be careful of was not showing the government in a bad light. Balanced reporting was a challenge – which, seeing as I was a former Reuters journalist, did somewhat irk me. However, I resigned myself to the fact that I was there to entertain the masses, not educate them. And after all, a population that couldn't have sex before marriage would need some serious distraction and entertainment.

As I left Freestyle that night, I couldn't help wondering if Miss Bopha had been making plans for an arranged marriage for me too.

I decided not to tell her about Amy.

THAI RIOTS

HAVING ESCAPED marriage and taken on the added responsibility of a new pet, I now had to turn my attention back to the TV channel. It was January, and Oknha was determined that we would go on air in March - with or without a studio building. In fact, he was so excited about the launch that he would call me up for updates at any time of the day or night.

"Where are you?" he would ask as I answered his late-night call.

There were never any 'hellos', 'how are yous' or 'am I disturbing you'. After a while, I figured that perhaps somebody in his past or in Australia had told him that 'where are you?' was an acceptable form of greeting – either that or he couldn't pronounce the word 'how', and he surmised that 'where' would do instead. Nevertheless, I got used to it.

"It's eleven o'clock, Oknha," I would reply. "I'm at home."

"How's the TV?"

"Fine, Oknha."

"Mmmmm, mmmm, mmmm," he would utter and ring off.

It was a fairly standard conversation. I was used to it by now.

However, this time, geopolitics got the better of us. The ever-present tensions between Cambodia and Thailand, somewhat akin to the love-hate relationship between France and Britain, suddenly came to the fore and reared their ugly heads.

In January 2003, a Thai actress was alleged to have said 'that she would not visit Cambodia until Angkor Wat was returned to Thailand'. This was picked up by the local press, who made a big deal of it.

As it was, the whole episode had been taken out of context. The Thai star Suvanant Kongying had never made the comments in person. They were in a script in a drama she was starring in and were unfairly attributed to her. At the time, this did not matter. Cambodian Prime Minister Hun Sen jumped on the bandwagon, saying that the actress was 'not worth a few blades of grass near the temple." This effectively gave the green light to those inclined to protest. And they did so – some violently. Students and youths went on a rampage, attacking the Thai embassy and Thai businesses. They also attacked our channel's competitors, TV5 and TV3.

Even before the violence had flared up, I started

receiving text messages demanding a boycott of Thai products. It was effectively spam but added to the tensions. I then saw Cambodian flag-waving youth parading around town on *motos*.

"What's all that about," I asked Mr. Bunthoeun.

"Oh, that? Nothing. Just a football match or something,"

A half-hour later, I drove past a mob gathering at the gates of the Thai embassy. The protesters waved placards and burnt tires. I could see the hostility on the agitators' faces through the palls of black smoke that rose delicately in the clear blue sky.

"Just a football match, eh?" I asked Bunthoeun over the phone. "It looks a bit nationalistic to me."

As an ex-Reuters journalist, I felt duty-bound to inform my former colleagues in the Reuters bureau. I put in a call to the expat bureau chief Dan.

"Are you reporting this?" I asked.

"No, it is all a misunderstanding," Dan replied.

"Misunderstanding?!? They are on the rampage!" I replied. I was confused with Mr. Bunthoeun and the Reuters bureau chief downplaying the situation. Perhaps my once well-honed journalistic instincts weren't quite what they used to be.

As it happened, I was proved wrong - about my instincts anyway. There was a problem. Within hours of my calling Reuters, the protesters had ransacked buildings, set fire to property and smashed furniture. It was serious stuff. The protesters had caused at least USD 6 million worth of damage to Thai-owned property. Hundreds of Thais living and working in Cambodia had to flee for their lives. The rage on the streets of Phnom Penh was palpable – and was not only directed at Thais.

Seeing what was happening and deciding there was no point galavanting about town, my mobile phone company colleague Kevin and I holed up at a bar. We had just sat down to some early evening beers and banter when the phone call came in.

"Sir, sir, we are at TV5," one of my new hires said excitedly.

Vannak was one of two Khmer staff that I had just poached from the TV channel TV5. He was a producer. The other was an editor called Nin. Despite signing on with our channel, they still lived on the TV5 compound. They were there when the irate Cambodian students began attacking the TV buildings – and their accommodation. They did so on the premise that TV5 ran Thai dramas.

"Is it dangerous?" I asked.

"Yes, Sir. We very scared."

"Ok, we will come and get you," I replied. "My friend Kevin will come with me."

When we reached Vannak and Nin, hundreds of rampaging students were out of control. It was as if the lid had been lifted off a pressure cooker, and the water had come to an angry, incessant, uncontrollable boil. There was tension all around.

In fact, as we neared the TV5 studio, I got out of the car. A group of students came running up to me.

"They burned down the Cambodian embassy in Bangkok!" someone shouted.

Actually, that particular accusation was a rumour. At this point in the evening, the riots had taken on a life of their own and were being driven by 'Chinese whispers' – on both sides of the border. There were stories about Cambodians defiling pictures of Thailand's revered King and reciprocal tales of Cambodians being attacked in Thailand. It was entirely out of control.

"What do you think about all this!?!" another student demanded aggressively.

"I don't think it should have happened," I replied, careful not to take any sides.

Kevin and I found Vannak and Nin and took them to my house. Once again, my guesthouse rooms would play host to stranded guests.

Content that Vannak and Nin were now safely settled at my place. Kevin and I returned to the bar to pick up where we had left off with beers and banter. We had invited my two house guests, but they declined to come.

And, then, another call.

"Sir, Sir, we are in jail. We are in army jail," Vannak announced.

"What!?! You're in a military jail!?! You're supposed to be at my place! How did that happen?"

"We do nothing wrong. We came back to look," Vannak replied meekly.

I turned to Kevin incredulously.

"They've been arrested. What is it with my place! No one ever seems to want to stay put! I think I'm going to get a revolving door installed!"

As it happened, we could not rescue Vannak and Nin; they spent a night in jail. It took Oknha's connections to get them out the next day.

"Next time they go to jail, they will stay there!" Oknha bellowed down the phone at me. "I am not doing it again."

The next time I saw Oknha, he had a new security adviser. He had a distinctly military gait. His name was Samnang.

While the Thai riots were terrible for Thai-Cambodia relations and the country's image, they were pretty good for us as a TV channel. In one fell swoop, the political upheaval took out our main competitor TV5. They had always relied heavily on Thai drama to dominate the ratings. Now, airing Thai dramas was a big no-no. Some people even thought our *Oknha* had a hand in starting the upheaval.

"Did Oknha start the riots?" I was often asked.

"Errr....no, even he does not have that power," I would reply.

Actually, he had a hand in rescuing some of the hapless Thai diplomats who had become stranded in their country's embassy. At our weekly meeting, Oknha recounted how he and Mr. Bunthoeun had to arrange their evacuation by boat along the river by smuggling them out of the embassy's back door. From there, he said, they were taken to waiting Thai air force transport planes.

There were actually hundreds of Thais who had been evacuated after Cambodians started attacking Thai businesses as well. Upon their arrival in Bangkok, the evacuees told stories about how the Cambodian police and army who escorted them to the airport stole their valuables.

As for us, with no Thai dramas to put on the air, we turned to the next best thing – Korean drama. We had already started building relations with Korean broadcasters and producers at the start of the decade-long 'Korean wave' when anything that came out of Seoul was all the rage.

SIEM REAP

Having witnessed first-hand the nationalistic fervour that the very mention of Angkor Wat had caused, I decided to make a trip to Siem Reap.

Ever since I arrived in Cambodia, I had heard ordinary Cambodians speak with reverence about their crown jewel Angkor Wat. And with the errant Jonno now overseeing the building of the studio complex, I took myself off to Siem Reap. It would be a short trip and a pleasant break from Phnom Penh.

As I left Lucky Villa early one morning, Cambodian Prime Minister Hun Sen's words – aimed at the Thai actress – were still ringing in my ears. The Prime Minister had said that the actress was 'not worth a few blades of grass near the temple', which, by all accounts, had added fuel to the already inflammatory situation that had sparked the riots.

As it happened, it was my second visit to the temple complex. The first took place in 2000 when I flew from Singapore for a few days. At that time, at least some of the 'blades of grass' that the prime minister spoke of still hid landmines, and certain parts of the park were still cordoned off. The mines were a hangover from the days of the Khmer Rouge. You were warned that you tread at your own risk.

I took the early morning domestic flight to Siem Reap. I arrived at about 8 am - which was late to start a morning excursion to the Angkor Wat temples. But I only had two days, so I would brave the heat and spend the day among the iconic spires and temples.

Hailing a taxi at the airport, my driver stopped, started and stuttered through the built-up part of Siem Reap on our way to our hotel. We headed toward the river - the town's epicentre. There, I would be staying at a quaint hotel with wooden bungalows and chalets.

Arriving at the hotel, I entered the windowless reception and headed for the front desk. I was told to sit on one of the rattan sofas littering the lobby and admired the old colonial decor there. There were Buddha statues and artefacts alongside paintings and sketches of Angkor Wat and Siem Reap in days gone by. Wooden walkways hovered over a picaresque pond that made up the 'grounds' of the hotel. White and pink lilies floated atop the jade-green water of the sprawling water feature. It made for a relaxing getaway.

By the time I had checked in, it was late morning. I dumped my case in the room, changed into hiking boots and rejoined my taxi driver, who would now act as my guide for the temples. He had upsold himself on the way from the airport.

The approach to the main temples at Angkor Wat was along a tree-lined boulevard. There, gibbons sat in wait as mini-buses and *motos* trundled past with camera-toting tourists eager to see the world's largest religious monument. As the iconic spires of Angkor Wat came into view, I held my breath once again. Even though I had seen Angkor Wat before, it was still awe-inspiring.

We parked in the dusty, unpaved parking lot across from the main temple. The spires loomed large in the clear blue Cambodian sky. Hundreds of visitors streamed back along the massive paved walkway that led from the main entrance to the west gate. I walked in the opposite direction towards the main temple.

Once inside, I wandered the cool corridors and marvelled at the friezes and inscriptions carved into the walls and pillars. I wondered at the attention to detail carved into the rock and the impressive stories of Angkor's heyday that they helped to unfold. I wondered at the enormity of the whole place and the intricate carvings and artwork that signalled the achievement and dominance of one of the world's greatest cultures. I thought about what had happened since.

Later on, I visited the many-faceted Bayon Temple and the more commercially renowned Ta Phrom - which had been made famous by Angelina Jolie in Tomb Raiders. Seeing them, I passed through the south gate of Angkor Thom, with its bridge adorned with sculpted heads depicting gods and demons.

"Miss Angelina come here to make a movie," my guard said excitedly. "She make our temple very famous. She also take care of Cambodian boy."

The boy my guide spoke of was Maddox, the Khmer youngster she had adopted when visiting an orphanage in the country. The adoption – and the movie – had done much to shine a light on Cambodia. And judging by the reaction of my guide as he proudly showed off what was considered the world's largest religious monument, ordinary Cambodians really did appreciate Angelina Jolie's attention.

As my guide told me – in somewhat broken English - Angkor consists of over 70 temples.

"They are from an ancient city that once housed one million people. Very big, Sir. Khmer very strong before," my guide explained.

And it was true, in days of old, the Khmer Empire was a force to be reckoned with.

"Now, different, Sir," the guard said wistfully.

Today, the guide went on, Angkor was still revered by ordinary Cambodians who still came to pay their respects. At the complex's centre was Angkor Wat, built in the 12th century to honour the Hindu god Vishnu. The guide explained how the temple's iconic towers, which were 60 metres in height, represented the mountain peaks believed to be the home of the gods.

"There are not many Khmers," I remarked.

"Too expensive to travel," the guide replied. "Road not so good and expensive to take taxi."

Towards sunset, we moved off to another temple to watch the sunset over Angkor Wat. We hiked up a dirt path to the top of a hill about a kilometre and a half away from Angkor Wat. As we walked, I became aware of an elephant walking alongside me. His keeper guided him, and a tourist sat on his back. The tourist had chosen the easy approach to Phnom Bakheng – content to let the elephant do the work.

This particular elephant reminded me of Sambo, who had become a Cambodian and Phnom Penh mainstay too. Sambo was an Asian elephant that strolled along Phnom Penh's riverside every evening. During the day, she could be found at the city's Wat Phnom – a Buddhist temple complex in the centre of Phnom Penh from which the city derived its name. There she, too, gave tourists rides.

Sambo's claim to fame was that she had survived the Khmer Rouge. However, she had five other siblings that were put to work by the Khmer Rouge – and didn't survive the ordeal. Sambo did.

Sambo's owner, who had been forced to hand her over to the Khmer Rouge when everything – and everyone – belonged to the state, heard that she had survived and came to retrieve her. He found her tied up in some mountain. She was said to be malnourished and weak. The owner brought her back to Phnom Penh.

During her time in Phnom Penh, Sambo was based at the city's Wat Phnom, where she was fed by visiting tourists. And then, every evening, she walked along the riverside, where she held her impressive trunk out to tourists as they sat in the boulevard's cafes. There they were encouraged to feed her bananas. While it might have been a happier lot than the elephant I saw before me now, there were certain similarities.

By early evening I had seen the sun setting over Angkor Wat and had dodged the scores of tourists taking their happy snaps. I had also seen enough of the park. I and my guide joined the lines of cars and vans that were now exiting the temple grounds. I sat back in my seat, soaked up the park's unique atmosphere, and peered out the windows at the gibbons as they preened and picked at one another under the trees. It had been a great day. And I hadn't seen any cordoned-off areas either. The landmines had been cleared.

My guide dropped me off at the hotel, and I tipped him generously. I then walked through the windowless wood-carved reception to my room. After a shower and changing clothes, I was ready for whatever Siem Reap nightlife had to offer. I headed to the Red Piano in the centre of town.

The Red Piano was a Siem Reap institution, just as the Foreign Correspondent Club was in Phnom Penh. And, as one would expect, the Red Piano was predominantly red. There were red walls and wicker chairs with red cushions. It was a comfortable place to sit to people-watch the tourists as they ambled along looking pink from their day's excursion at Angkor. I whiled away a couple of hours sipping beers as tourists wandered to and fro, looking for somewhere to dine.

I had seen Siem Reap, Angkor Wat and the temples that had caused the riots.

HERE'S TO BENNY HILL

I PUT the TV channel on air on March 8th 2003. We went on air without a studio, and so, like HBO or Cinemax, much of our output consisted of dubbed dramas, Ripley's Believe It or Not, Mr. Bean and even Benny Hill. In fact, Benny Hill was our inaugural program.

It was a Thursday when we went on air, and the plan was to launch with news – which, considering my Reuters background, should have been a doddle. The idea was to make a splash. In 2003, international news on TV still consisted of the BBC headlines translated and dubbed into Khmer. It was amusing to see the likes of Moira Stewart delivering the news in Khmer - so to speak.

So, thinking that we would impress the audience with homegrown news, we compiled a bulletin consisting of the exploits of Oknha and the considerable investment in Cambodia's brand-new nationwide television channel and the media industry in general. It was an hour's worth of pure unadulterated self-aggrandisement in which Oknha was the undisputed star. There was also some international news that we got from Reuters.

However, just minutes before we went on air, our main edit suite, where we were putting the finishing touches to our inaugural news program, froze – as did the editor.

I cajoled, encouraged, and pleaded – but was careful not to raise my voice and cause panic and laughter as I paced behind our news video editor. He sweated and coughed nervously and clicked his mouse furiously to no avail. Our state-of-the-art editing system had fallen at the last hurdle and had packed up completely.

"Run Benny!" I shouted desperately at the technicians in the control room. "Run Benny!"

The technicians looked at me questioningly, wondering whether the pointy-nosed foreigner had finally succumbed to the pressure and ultimately lost his mind. After all, the crazy *barang* asked them to replace one of Cambodia's richest and most powerful men with a bumbling, stumbling, chubby, red-faced British comedian racing around a field chasing scantily-clad beauties. No doubt they also wondered what the Prime Minister's wife Bun Rany would make of it - seeing as she was a staunch advocate of respecting the female form.

"Don't worry," I said soothingly to put their horror-stricken minds to rest. "Oknha will understand."

We went on air - with Benny.

Then came the call, "Where are you?"

"At the control room, Oknha."

I prepared for the worst. I prepared for whatever Oknha was about to throw at me. Instead, he threw me with his line of questioning.

"What's the matter with the sound?" Oknha asked stoically. "It's too low."

"It's the international standard. We are monitoring the levels," I replied as I glanced at the audio levels.

"It's low," Oknha replied. "Anyway, I need you to put something on the air. I'll tell you at our next meeting."

"What's that?" I asked.

"I'll tell you at our next meeting," Oknha repeated and rung off.

At the next meeting at the top of the Cambodiana Hotel, Mr. Bunthoeun handed me a tape.

"Don't question... don't argue. Just broadcast it," Oknha instructed.

Back at the control centre, I looked at the tape. I saw hundreds of animated Khmer men jockeying for position around a piece of dirt. In the centre were two irate cockerels going hell-for-leather at each others' throats. It was cock-fighting. The men watching were jeering and shouting, and Khmer riel banknotes exchanged hands with every stab and peck. The Cambodians considered it sport. It was popular with gamblers. The tape had come from the deputy prime minister. He owned chicken farms.

We also stole Premier League football from TV5 because they broke matches by placing TV commercials. This was forbidden. By placing TV commercials as such, the at-home audience risked missing goals, penalties, or major incidents on the pitch. Using my connections at ESPN in Singapore, I reported them for breach of contract. ESPN reacted by giving us the whole season's matches. You had to be ruthless while running TV channels, I was learning. It was a competitive field.

Kickboxing also formed part of our sports line-up. We would sometimes take over a local stadium and stage international bouts. And while all TV channels ran kickboxing and international bouts, I turned ours into team kickboxing. I did so because I couldn't find any sports that Cambodia excelled at, at the time - apart from kickboxing.

The only real difference between our team kickboxing and others' regular kickboxing was the packaging. We would assemble a team of three French kickboxers against Cambodian kickboxers and then match up the fighters. Each boxer would fight his own bout against his opponent but would represent his country. At the end of the event, we would tally up the wins and losses and pronounce the winner – which was invariably Cambodia. We brought in Americans, New Zealanders and Australians - and most of them lost. The Cambodian audience loved it - and so did the Prime Minister.

We promoted the fights to such an extent that ninety per cent of the population could not help but watch – including the Prime Minister himself. During the fights, representatives of the prime minister would call in with offers of thousands of dollars of bonuses for winners and losers alike. The prime minister's office would offer one thousand dollars to the Cambodian if he won – and then also offer five hundred dollars to the foreigner if he did. And since the Prime Minister had donated money, all the other tycoons would follow suit. They took the PM's lead. It was a way of ingratiating themselves with the government and the public alike.

Often, we would have to hold up the fights between rounds to allow everyone to call in. After all, our sports presenter Ma Serey had to take to the microphone in the middle of the ring and relay all the donations to the audience in the stands and at home watching TV.

"Glen, the foreign trainers are complaining?" our South African promoter Paddy informed me on one occasion as we stood on a raised platform overlooking the ring. "They think you're buying time for the Khmers because they're out of shape. The foreigners are fitter."

"Paddy, what do you want me to do? Hang up on the Prime Minister? They will have to wait."

And wait, they did. But they weren't happy.

When we invited a team of three Americans to fight three Khmers, Paddy presented me with a photo of an American kickboxer for use in our marketing materials. He was a Rastafarian, and he sported dreadlocks in keeping with his religion.

"Paddy, the guy looks like he's homeless. What do you think the Cambodians will make of this?" I asked. "I need a better picture, or I'll photoshop it."

And so I did. I naively lopped off Mike's dreadlocks, not realising that I was now tampering with his Rastafarian religion and belief.

Despite the pictorial haircut and damaged pride, Mike put in an excellent showing against one of Cambodia's star kickboxers Eh Phutong. Eh Phutong was the undisputed Cambodian champion and pride of Cambodia. The mere mention of his name caused any ordinary Cambodian to bristle with pride.

"Jeez, that guy can kick like a mule!" Mike the Rastafarian said after facing him in the ring. Mike had put up a good showing but had ultimately lost. He was gracious in defeat.

While we were able to bring foreign boxers to Cambodia, in 2003, we couldn't bring Thais. It was just too sensitive.

"If it is a disputed result, we will have a riot," Oknha said when I suggested we do Cambodia vs. Thailand. "It won't work."

And that was that. Cross-border politics was now front and centre in Cambodia's most famous pastime too.

"And make sure your foreign boxers don't have *Muay Thai* on their shorts," Oknha added.

Muay Thai means Thai boxing, so it was an anathema to the Khmers, whose own version of kickboxing was called *Khun Khmer*.

It was explained to me that it would be as if we took the humble game of 'football' and started calling it 'French Football', allowing the 'beautiful game' to become the de facto property of the French. The British and the rest of the world would not appreciate it.

I thought back to the Thai riots. I got the point.

SHOWKIE

WHILE I WAS busy launching the TV channel, Showkie, was rapidly transforming himself from a Cambodian street dog into a domesticated pet. He took to Seila and Miss Bopha immediately. Then he warmed to me after he realised I was responsible for putting food on his plate – or at least in his bowl.

He developed a real hankering for cheese. I put it down to the fact that after Miss Bopha had retired for the night, I would sneak into the kitchen and make myself a cheese sandwich. And while standing at the fridge door, I would reach in, break off a piece of cheddar and hand it to him. He would immediately grab it from me, turn on his heel, run to his favourite spot, flop on his blanket, and happily gulp the morsel down. He did the same with bread, which soon became another favoured treat.

I also put in place a strict regime of walks which, as a Cambodian street dog, he was not at all used to. Most of Cambodia's pet owners seemed reluctant to walk their dogs.

Instead, they preferred keeping the animal in the house or the garden. And then, when the dog needed exercise, they let their pet wander around at will in the street outside. So, when I informed Seila that he had a newfound responsibility, he was somewhat taken aback. He even asked for a pay raise.

"Let's see how you do first," I replied.

To alleviate Seila's concerns about his new role as a dog walker, I took the lead – literally and figuratively. I took Showkie for his first-ever walk as Seila stood at the gate and watched as our Khmer neighbours snickered at what they considered crazy pet pampering.

'Oiiii! You have a lucky dog!" one of my neighbours shouted.

"Showkie like a king!" another called out.

Taking Showkie for his first-ever walk proved more challenging than I ever imagined. To begin with, he was reticent about leaving what had now become his home. And being as territorial as he was, as soon as I attached the lead, he promptly plonked his bum down on the asphalt drive and refused to budge. I couldn't help thinking that he thought that his cushy new lifestyle had ended abruptly and that he was being turned out on his ear. After all, much like our Khmer neighbours, the concept of him going for a walk had probably never entered his canine mind.

At first, I tried to encourage him. And then I decided to bribe him by waving bread and cheese in front of him. He gobbled up the cheddar and the sliced bread but still wouldn't budge. Finally, I dragged him unceremoniously out into the street, scraping his bum along the drive as I did so. However, he wasn't happy. He strained at the leash and kept whipping his head around to watch our home and Seila, who was still standing watch at the gate, getting smaller and smaller as we walked further and further into the world outside our house.

When we turned our first corner, we came across another street dog. The mongrel belonged to one of the families living in the houses nearby. And like many other Cambodian pets, it was left to roam the streets by itself without any due care, attention, or concern for who it might bark at or bite.

Even though this particular Cambodian street dog was more petite than Showkie, he had a more ferocious temperament and bark. As soon as he saw Showkie, he went for him. Instead of putting up a fight as I would have liked Showkie to do, my dog promptly pulled up and peed on himself in fright. Having made a spectacle of himself to the neighbourhood and cowed in the face of smaller opposition, Showkie sat down in surrender in the same spot where he had just urinated. Realising that Showkie would not fend for himself or me, I swung a few kicks in the general direction of our assailant - without connecting - and then turned and started for home, much to Showkie's relief.

The first thing I did when I got inside my gate was to order Seila to wash Showkie to clean off his yellow dog pee, and then I marched to the kitchen at the back of the house to have a word with Miss Bopha.

"Where did you get Showkie?" I asked.

"He street dog. He like me a lot. He used to follow me to market," she replied.

"He's not very brave for a street dog," I remarked.

"Outside, he polite. Inside his territory. You wait. You just wait and see how he guards territory."

As it happened, I didn't have to wait long to find out just how territorial Showkie could be. It happened when I had my first-ever barbeque at home. It was my first time inviting office and mobile phone company friends. And, of course, Bradley and Jean were among them.

Miss Bopha had come in on her day off. She arranged a fantastic spread that included green chicken curry, spare ribs, glass noodle salad and the local speciality fish amok. There was also the barbeque, which was my responsibility – and the ice chest full of beers and wine.

It was a Saturday evening, and everyone started arriving at sundown - at about six thirty. The sky had turned orange, as it was wont to do at that time of year, and hardly a cloud was in sight.

I was nervous, and so was Showkie. Miss Bopha, on the other hand, was the picture of calm. I couldn't help thinking that maybe she had been a French Embassy chef after all. She seemed to be used to catering for guests.

We all took to our posts whenever a new guest arrived at the gate. I opened the gate, Seila held back Showkie, and Miss Bopha presented a tray of beers and wines to ensure everyone had a welcome drink upon arrival. It was all going well – until Bradley and Jean appeared. Then, Showkie slipped from Seila's not-so-commanding grasp and went for

Jean. He rushed at her, nipped her on the leg and went scampering off up the drive.

"Seila!" I shouted at the top of my lungs. "Get him before he gets somebody else."

"Yes, Sir," Seila called back halfway up the drive.

"Don't worry, Jean," I said, turning to her and Bradley as they surveyed the wound. "It was just a love bite."

Bradley and Jean understood that I was trying to make light of it, but Showkie's nip had drawn blood, and they both looked somewhat concerned.

"He has had his rabies injections, I hope?" Bradley said.

"Of course, I'm sure he has," I replied hesitantly.

"You don't sound that sure. I think you had best check," Bradley countered.

I phoned the vet only to find out that his rabies injections were out of date. The vet said he had tried to call to remind me, but there was no response. He thought I had moved and had given up. It turned out that he had the wrong number listed.

"I think you should bring Jean in for the injections," the vet advised helpfully. "Or she can wait to see if the dog dies – and if it does, we will cut the head off and check if it had rabies."

I put the vet's suggestion to Bradley and Jean.

"Has he been bitten by a rat or another dog?" Bradley asked.

"Not to my knowledge."

"Well, I'll take my chances," Jean replied.

With that, Showkie was banished indoors, where he stood barking at the door for twenty minutes before giving up and collapsing in a heap. We continued with our barbeque, and by the time it was nine in the evening, everyone had forgotten the excitement of the hours before. However, over the next few weeks, Bradley would ask with persistent regularity after Showkie's welfare.

"He's still alive," I would respond.

"Good, I'll inform Jean," Bradley would smile.

While Bradley and Jean appeared relaxed about the whole Showkie episode, I was somewhat peeved. I set about investigating who had been remiss at not getting the requisite shots. It turned into a three-way discussion between Miss Bopha, Seila and myself. And as usual, Miss Bopha had the last word.

"I bring you Showkie to make you responsible!" Miss Bopha announced. "Next time, I bring you something stronger!"

With that as a parting shot, Miss Bopha stormed into the kitchen, leaving me staring at Seila's blank face. He was as puzzled as I was.

"What does she mean by that?" I asked.

"I don't know, Sir."

I silently considered the possibility of returning home from work the next day to find an ox or a bullock tethered to a post in my drive. After all, plenty of them were in the paddies that made up the Cambodian countryside around Phnom Penh.

HITTING THE ROAD...AND OTHER THINGS THAT CAME ALONG

HEAD OFFICE finally relented about the studio, and Oknha got his wish. He was elated and started planning a grand opening.

"Samdech has to open a state-of-the-art facility," Oknha announced, using the Prime Minister's official title. "It is good for him because it shows he is bringing serious investment to the country. It is also good for us because it shows that we are serious about investing in Cambodia. Then we will get more licences and more opportunities."

Content that he was getting his state-of-the-art studio to match the hi-tech control rooms and playout facilities that we had already invested in, Oknha would often summon me and Bradley and some of the other expats to dinners and drinks sessions and signing ceremonies where other *oknhas* and dignitaries were present. Invariably, the progress of the brand-new studio was brought up.

"Let's see the pictures," Oknha would ask as I unfolded my laptop and opened studio design mock-up folders. There then followed some audible sighs of satisfaction and some sing-song Khmer as some dignitary or another congratulated Oknha on getting the *barangs* to bend to his wishes and build an expensive studio.

With our station now on air – even without a studio, I found that I had to attend more and more meetings outside, and I also had to drive between our broadcast centre and the studio. And although I had a driver, I found that the best way to get around was by driving myself. The local drivers provided by the company were just too careful and cautious to be of any use to me whatsoever. Like Oknha's driver Mr. Ratanak, they travelled at a top speed of thirty kilometres an hour. But the comparison stopped there. Unlike Mr. Ratanak, my drivers were usually always in the wrong place at the wrong time or getting lost on Phnom Penh's pot-holed back streets. With this in mind, I elected to drive myself.

Driving in downtown Phnom Penh was not for the faint-hearted. There was all manner of traffic - four-wheeled, two-wheeled, two-legged - and even four-legged - travelling in every possible direction on almost any stretch of road, pavement, grass or forecourt. The rules of the road simply didn't apply – and neither did the authority of the city's questionable police force.

Driving through downtown Phnom Penh on any given day, you could reasonably expect to see entire families of four mounted on two-wheeled *motos*, groups of up to twelve people crammed into unofficial Toyota Camry taxis and thirty or so garment factory workers standing bolt-upright in the backs of rusty and dilapidated flatbed trucks. You could also sometimes see monkeys chained to the bonnet or backs of cars as they crawled on all fours over the moving vehicles. And then, taking pride of place on Sisowath Quay every evening was an elephant named Sambo who took her evening stroll along the riverside, poking her formidable trunk into the sidewalk cafes in the hopes of being fed a banana or two by bemused tourists.

"Don't think about it. Just get on and do it," Bradley had advised when I mentioned that I might drive myself around town.

And so, with Bradley as a role model and a Land Rover Discovery provided by the company, I began driving myself to meetings and out and about around town.

To begin with, things were fine. I found that, despite unruly appearances, most of Phnom Penh's cars, trucks and *motos* could skirt around one another happily - if not haphazardly. Roundabouts, however, provided a real challenge. Everyone seemed to drive headlong at one another before executing a last-minute swerving manoeuvre to get out of harm's way.

As for the city's police, well, their only role appeared to be to step out into the road in front of oncoming traffic, waving down drivers and demanding money for the slightest infraction - whether it endangered other vehicles or pedestrians or not. The city's traffic police seemed to have no influence on whether drivers followed road rules or whether the traffic flowed smoothly or not. Instead, their self-designated lot in life was merely to collect money which they then put in their own pockets rather than the government's coffers. They were particularly active at the end of every month after spending their meagre salaries on beer and girls.

On the few occasions I had run-ins with the police, I would stop, trade some banter and pay a few dollars before heading off. It was always a good-natured transaction that generally started with a policeman stepping out into the road, waving me down and then asking to see my licence. Once he had seen my documents, he would then ask for ten dollars. I would laugh and say that the amount requested was far too much. I would then offer a dollar per policeman, which would be accepted by their designated police negotiator - usually the one with the best English. Having paid my bribe, I would smile, wave, and head off into the city's motorised mayhem.

"Make sure you only pay one dollar a policeman," someone had warned. "We don't want you ruining it for the rest of us. If you pay more, we'll have to pay the same. You'll create inflation."

However, on one occasion, I did pay more. It involved an accident when I travelled to our hi-tech broadcast facility, which was slightly out of town. It was not just a run-of-the-mill scrape. It was a pretty solid whack.

As I was making my way up Norodom Boulevard, a *moto* stopped dead in its tracks right in front of me. The driver had given absolutely no indication or warning. He just stopped.

Whether he had broken down or just wanted to cross the road, I wasn't quite sure at the time. It all happened so fast, and I had little time to think. I slammed on the brakes, shouted a Khmer expletive through a closed window and skidded to a standing stop. I sighed in relief as I looked around to find that all was well with me - and the offending *moto* in front of me too.

I was still congratulating myself on my keen reflexes when I felt the solid whack and crump of something in the back. Shocked by the collision, I turned to see two teenagers reeling and wobbling unsteadily in the middle of the road behind me. As I peered through the dust on my Landrover Discovery window, I noticed that the teenagers looked dazed, concussed, or both. They also looked as if they were about to collapse in a crumpled, gangly-legged heap in the middle of the street at any moment.

The two punch-drunk figures continued reeling around in the middle of the road. They were young men who had been travelling two to a bike. They had been speeding and dodging in and out of traffic.

While part of me felt sorry for them - and the fact that they had run headlong into the back of me - another part of me thought that they had got what they deserved. After all, these were the type of 'wide boy' youngsters I called 'boy-racers'. Their modus operandi was to whip in and out of traffic and drive along the wrong side of the street while carrying on an animated conversation among themselves. They were a menace to themselves and all about them.

Somewhat startled by the violence of the impact, I pondered my options. Should I get out and help? Should I drive to the side of the road and ask for help from passersby? Should I press on? In the end, I called our Mr. Fixit Srun.

"Where are you, Sir?" Srun asked. "Are there any police around?"

"Takhmau, and no, there are no police here", I replied, unsure if that was a good or a bad thing.

"Sir, keep driving," Srun insisted.

"What?"

"Keep driving, Sir. Please," Srun pleaded. "People may be no good, Sir. Maybe you hurt their children, their brother. Maybe they're angry."

Although it went against every instinct I had to leave two injured youngsters careering around in the middle of the street, I followed Srun's advice. Without police, a crowd could turn into a mob, and innocent bystanders could suddenly turn to violence. It had been known to happen. In fact, there were regular reports of villagers and onlookers taking the law into their own hands and beating guilty parties to death for injuring their friends and relatives. At that point, I remembered my jaunt around town a year before and talk about lynching. I moved off.

I only drove another fifteen minutes before a policeman stepped onto the road and flagged me down.

"Oh, come on, not now," I said to myself, thinking it would involve the usual practice of demanding money.

It wasn't. Instead, I was whisked off to a nearby police station, where a sombre-looking official questioned me for the best part of two hours. During this time, I was joined by Samnang - Oknha's new security advisor. He had been given a job after rescuing Vannak and Nin from jail. He was the one with the distinctly military gait. I smiled when I saw him.

Despite Samnang's best efforts to plead my case, and even though the boy racers had hit me, I paid the fine. It cost the company one thousand dollars to cover the youngsters' hospital bills and to repair their crumpled *moto*.

"Big cars always pay for little cars or bikes," Samnang explained as we stepped out of the police station into the mid-afternoon sun. "Besides, I think he liked you."

"Liked me? He charged me – us, the company - one thousand dollars," I replied.

"Yes, but you *barang*," Samnang smiled. "He could have charged you more and made a bigger problem."

As for my car, it escaped unscathed, save for a slight dent in the backdoor frame. When I looked at it closely, I swore I could see the imprint of one of the boy racer's faces chiselled into the metalwork. With that in mind, I asked to change cars. I didn't want to be reminded of my mishap when loading my shopping, luggage or other items into the back. As a result, I ended up with a Toyota Rav 4. It was lighter and more suited to the erratic pace of Phnom Penh's traffic. It also went reasonably fast.

Once I had taken delivery of the new car, I took Miss Bopha out for a spin. She wanted to visit some relatives in Kampong Chhnang, and I was happy to see something of the Cambodian countryside. It would make a change from spending a weekend within the confines of the capital.

Kampong Chhnang was on a mostly flat road about two hours north of Phnom Penh. On the way out of town, we drove past our studio building, a Cham Moslem suburb of the city with mosques dotted along the roadside, and Cham women with headscarves moving to and fro.

Once away from the city and the suburbs, I opened my new car up, reaching speeds of about sixty kilometres per hour – which was fast for Cambodia. I turned up the volume on my CD player and put my foot down even further. I pushed the little 4x4 to about seventy kilometres an hour, nearly as fast as I wanted to go on the broken, uneven, pot-holed roads that led away from town.

As we neared a bend, I saw Miss Bopha clutching her handbag to her chest, her face was ash-white, and she had knuckles to match. She appeared to be squeezing the pink hue out of her clenched fingers and was rigid with fear. She stared straight ahead through the window and winced as cars, houses, and trees loomed before us. When she caught me looking at her, she glanced at me sideways and then returned her attention to the road.

"Miss Bopha, are you OK?" I asked.

"Why do you drive so fast?" she asked, annoyed.

"Well, it's a two-hour drive," I replied. "You will want time to spend with your relatives, no?"

"Yes, but Miss Bopha don't want an accident," she replied, her eyes still wide with fear. "Miss Bopha survive Khmer Rouge. Miss Bopha not want to die on the road to Kampong Chhnang. Miss Bopha want to see relatives - not relatives see Miss Bopha in box."

By box, she meant coffin. So, suitably reprimanded, I slowed down. I had forgotten that cars and trucks were a relatively new phenomenon to those like Miss Bopha, who had been forced to work in the countryside by the Khmer Rouge. When I had reduced the speed to forty kilometres per hour, Miss Bopha gave an audible sigh of relief. She began to survey the scenery around her. She gave a little bow as we passed Mount Oudong and its Buddhist temple. I wasn't sure if she was giving thanks for my slowing down or praying I wouldn't speed up again. Whichever it was, she seemed much more relaxed, and the colour returned to her weather-beaten face and pale knuckles.

On another occasion, I drove to Sihanoukville. After spending an enjoyable time at the beach with great weather and good friends, it came time to depart. However, enjoying the company and the ambience as I was, I elected to leave late. I started out just as it was getting dark. It was a decision I began to regret almost as soon as I was a dozen or so kilometres up the road.

After driving for half an hour, the street lights suddenly disappeared, and the world outside my Rav 4 window turned pitch black. It was also then that I came upon truck after truck careering past me, alongside me or in front of me, some with broken tail lights and others with unlit steel metal girders protruding off their flatbed backs. I had to peer into the night beyond my windscreen to make out the distorted shapes as they loomed before me. It took every ounce of concentration, and my eyes and head hurt with the effort.

Only after about an hour into the journey did I realise

why the truck drivers insisted on blinding their fellow drivers with their 'brights'. And it wasn't malicious or selfish, contrary to what I had first suspected. Instead, they wanted to avoid hitting the villagers who sat on the road – not by the side of the road, but actually on the road, in the road! The local villagers appeared content to take their lives into their own hands by turning the side of the road into their public makeshift open-air living rooms. Apparently, it was cooler there - with the breeze created by close-passing traffic.

The villagers were dark-skinned and stripped to the waist and, as a result, were very difficult to see on the unlit motorway. It made for an exhausting three-and-a-half-hour drive back to the capital – for the truck drivers who continued to hurtle past and me.

When I finally got back to Phnom Penh, I reconsidered my decision of not having a driver - especially on long journeys, like to Sihanoukville. On short journeys between the broadcast centre and the soon-to-be-finished studio, I would drive myself.

ALL CREATURES GREAT AND SMALL...AND FISH PASTE TOO

WHILE DRIVING AROUND, I saw all manner of creatures on the roads around Phnom Penh. Buffaloes and cows wandered in the middle of the road as geese, chickens, and even gibbons inhabited Phnom Penh's boulevards.

One day I saw some creatures scrabbling around on the back of a car. They were not in the car. They were actually on it. As I neared the vehicle, I peered hard. There, running around on the bonnet and boot, were monkeys. They were chained to the car and seemed to be going about their business quite happily, irrespective of the fact that they were in perennial motion and were travelling at the motorist's top speed of thirty kilometres per hour.

As for myself, I was peering so intently at the gibbons that I forgot my place on the thoroughfare and almost ran into the back of a dilapidated Toyota Camry full to the brim with people and luggage. It was a close call.

In downtown Phnom Penh I would see gibbons doing a highwire act on various electricity cables and pylons. They also populated pagodas and parks and were a regular feature on several streets, with tourists disregarding the danger and the fact that monkeys are a particular nuisance and insisting on feeding them. It was the same at the entrance to Angkor Wat, where they added to the exotic ambience.

Other regular sights on the streets of Phnom Penh included pigs, squashed together like sardines in crates with wire mesh, on their way to market. I was told that their owners got them drunk before loading them up on their *motos* or pickups on the understanding that by being drunk, they are less prone to suffering stress – which is bad for the taste of the meat, apparently.

I also saw chickens strapped together on the backs of *motos*. Their clawed feet were invariably strapped to a piece of wood, and they dangled head-down with their beaks mere inches from the tarmac or dirt road on which they were travelling. By being transported in this manner, the seller could assure prospective buyers that the meat was fresh. They arrived at the market live.

With a premium being put on the freshness of food in Cambodia, a visit to any Khmer market would turn the stomach of any animal rights activist or, indeed, any ordinary mortal. Cambodia's markets regularly featured frogs that had been skinned alive – with some still being alive when they were put on display. Fish were still alive, flopping around in waterless buckets and containers. And, as for prawns, they were even brought to the dinner table still squirming – and still alive. A skewer had been inserted between their shell and body, and they were destined to be dunked in steaming hot broth. Again, dinner guests could be assured that their dinner really was fresh. But it wasn't for the squeamish.

As for wildlife, there were persistent instructions not to eat or trade bushmeat or wildlife. Whether they were adhered to or abided by was anybody's guess.

Cambodia's national animal was the kouprey – a kind of ox inhabiting forests with long horns. Other animals included water buffaloes and deer. Cambodia's wildlife also comprises bears, tigers, elephants, panthers, cormorants, cranes, ibises, parrots, green peafowl, pheasants, and wild ducks. And then there were snakes of the venomous and constricting variety. Personally I had seen the odd elephant and plenty of water buffalo as well as an occasional snake - but that was about it.

Poaching was rife in 2003, and at least some of Cambodia's animals were destined for the dinner table. After surviving the Khmer Rouge, Cambodians were not generally concerned with what they ate - as long as they did eat. And furthermore, some creatures that we considered off-limits in the West were usually palatable in Cambodia,

Take insects and spiders, for example. Crickets, ants, grasshoppers, cicadas, silkworm pupae and a variety of beetle grubs were eaten as snacks - as were tarantula spiders! In fact, the tarantulas were a delicacy. It wasn't a fad. It was a staple food.

I used to think that Khmers had a taste for bugs and crickets because of their unfortunate past. During the Khmer Rouge years eating such insects kept them alive. And even though that might have been the case, as it turned out, ordinary Khmers hankered for such morsels.

On any given evening, an insect seller could pitch up at a

table with a wicker basket full of fried crickets. And instead of turning up their noses in disgusts, young Cambodians would gather around the seller only to emerge with a handful of crickets. It was the same in Thailand.

When I asked about the practice of selling spiders, I was told Tarantulas can fetch about 10 cents each. Sellers normally can expect to sell 100 and 200 a day, so the venture definitely 'has legs', so to speak. A good tarantula seller could expect to make a few hundred dollars monthly. It was not a bad living at that particular juncture of Cambodia's evolution.

And how does a tarantula taste? I'm told it is a cross between a chicken and a fish. And the head and legs are somewhat crunchy - as one might expect. But, having not eaten one myself, I could not say much more than that.

Slightly more appetising and more prevalent was *prahok*. *Prahok* is Cambodia's distinctive fermented fish paste, a nutritious condiment produced at the end of the rainy season.

With our TV tower being on land bordering the Tonle Sap, I had smelt a lot of it – and would smell even more during my tenure as head of the TV channel.

Prahok was usually produced towards the end of the rainy season and was a way for fishermen and riverbank dwellers to store the fish for the rest of the year.

It is usually used as a condiment but is packed with taste and nutrition. It is sometimes given to the poor and needy to provide them with sustenance.

To make *prahok*, one dries dead fish in baskets outdoors for 24 hours. During this time, the fish begins to rot – and reek. Then the rotting produce is marinated in stacks of salt before being pounded together to form a paste. Then the paste is placed into containers with another dose of salt before being stored for a month. The result is a condiment that stinks to high heaven but can be used in Cambodia's kitchens for the rest of the year.

Cambodians are particularly proud of *prahok* as a national dish. And in some homes, no meal would be complete without it. The dish has been around since ancient times and can be stored for up to three years.

My erstwhile colleagues swore by it. They used it to flavour soups and vegetables.

"*Prahok*, Sir?" I would often be asked as I sat down at a table with staff.

"Errrr....no, thanks," I would politely reply.

"*Prahok* very tasty," Sreng or Vannak or Nin would say.

"Yes, I am sure it is, but taste good enough," I would continue.

"*Prahok* taste same same like your cheese, Sir," I was regularly informed.

Nevertheless, I held fast and declined the offer of *Prahok* for years. The stench was enough for me. Come the end of the rainy season, there was plenty of that in the atmosphere surrounding our studio.

And, whenever I went to dinner in Cambodia - with Oknha or otherwise, I never asked what was on the menu. I preferred not to know. When it came to eating in Cambodia, ignorance really was bliss.

As it happened, as we were waiting for the studio, there were dinner parties, grand openings, MOU signings, and other assorted events.

We would assemble in a Chinese restaurant and gather around a circular table where the food gyrated around a lazy susan. There were river prawns served still alive and kicking and often squirming on skewers that protruded from beneath their shell-like skin. Then there were black chickens with beaks, heads and shiny eyes dunked and boiled in a clear broth. There were also more mundane dishes like steamed sea bass stuffed with almonds and lemon and suckling pigs splayed belly-down on silver platters. These culinary mainstays were served alongside other dishes I couldn't identify - and I didn't dare to ask what they were.

When we weren't at a Chinese or Asian restaurant, we would go to an upmarket French restaurant. Oknha rubbed shoulders with the city's elite, including competitor tycoons and ministers. We knocked back the best champagne and liqueurs and commented on the vintage as if we knew what we were drinking. It made for an expensive evening out - for Oknha and ultimately for Bradley and the head office.

"Consider it business development," Oknha would say when questions over the substantial bills arose.

Oknha fended off Bradley's and the company's protestations about the entertainment expenses. After all, for Oknha, it was all about face. He simply couldn't be seen drinking ordinary bottles of wine amid such salubrious gatherings. It would reflect poorly on himself and the company. Like any Asian businessman, face played a massive part in wining, dining and general entertaining.

There were similar conversations about bodyguard and driver expenses too. But Oknha's argument was not just about face. It was also about self-preservation.

"They are there to save my life. How can I question their expenses when they could be risking their lives?" Oknha would argue.

In carrying out his business, Oknha invariably involved me – or some other hapless *barang* on his or another partner company's payroll. We were wheeled out to impress whoever Oknha might be entertaining - in whatever nightclub or karaoke parlour they ended up in.

At first, Oknha didn't really drink himself. He employed others to do that for him. One who always looked the worse for wear was Mr. Bunthoeun. I could always tell if there was a meaningful business connection in town just by the pallor of Bunthoeun's complexion or the number of aspirin he was downing with his morning coffee. And even though he always put a brave face on it, I knew he had had a raucous one in some nightclub or karaoke parlour the night before.

After we had been on the air for a few months, Oknha began developing a taste for fine wines and whisky. At first, it was wine, but then he graduated to whisky, which was the tipple of choice for the generals and other holders of the keys to the Kingdom – or the keys to the security and customs posts at the nation's borders.

Unlike the ministers, with whom Oknha regularly wined and dined, the generals did not have a refined palate. For them, it was all about getting as drunk as possible as fast as possible and then heading to a discreet karaoke joint to cavort with some young Cambodian ladies. And since Oknha needed them and their authority over the country's borders, ports and motorways, Oknha had to play along. In Oknha's world, getting drunk was not so much a leisure pursuit as a means to an end. This end usually meant buying influence, acquiring permissions or obtaining a licence. In Cambodia's business community, it wasn't so much what you knew as who you knew – and exactly how much you were prepared to pay to wine and dine those with influence.

On one occasion, Bradley and I were waiting for a meeting with Oknha at the business lounge at the Cambodiana Hotel. It was 3 pm in the afternoon.

"Oknha wants you at the nightclub," Mr. Bunthoeun announced. The club to which Mr. Bunthoeun referred belonged to Oknha's relative. It was newly opened, consisting of a large dance floor and upstairs karaoke rooms.

"But it's mid-afternoon...." Bradley protested.

"Oknha insists."

And that was that. Our afternoon appointment had been moved to one of the most raucous nightspots in the city.

"This is going to involve whisky, Bradley, "I said. "I hope you don't have a conference call with the head office this afternoon."

We were ushered into a darkened karaoke room at the top of the stairs at Oknha's relative's club. Khmer pop favourites were blasting from the speakers. A rotund Bhudda-like figure was seated on the plush velvet-cushioned seat placed ten feet from the big screen TV. He had a dark-haired, skimpily-clad beauty on either side of him, and he swooned into a microphone.

"Top general," Mr. Bunthoeun whispered knowingly as we entered the room.

No sooner had Mr. Bunthoeun spoken when Bradley and I were grabbed by the elbows and frog-marched to stand in front of the all-important general. A uniformed officer stood on either side of us. They each reached for a glass and a bottle of whisky and poured four fingers of whisky into our respective tumblers.

"Drink!" they shouted in unison, and as instructed, Bradley and I downed our drinks. We were whisked out of the way so the general could return to his singing. Bradley and I regrouped a few seats down on the plush velvet-cushioned bench seating that lined the walls.

Bradley and I were hauled in front of the general another four times. By the time I had drained my fourth glass, my head was spinning – and so was Bradley's. Needless to say, no company business was discussed that day.

Later I asked Mr. Buntoeun who the uniformed figure was.

"He is one of the most powerful men in the Kingdom," Mr. Bunthoeun replied stoically. "Apart from the prime minister, of course."

"He is the head of the national police force," Mr. Bunthoeun added.

As it happened, 'one of the most powerful men' in the Kingdom died in a helicopter crash in a storm some years later. There were allegations of foul play.

On another occasion, I took a visiting Reuters ex-colleague on an excursion to Phnom Penh's lively nightlife. In doing so, I ended up at the Lounge on the city's Sisowath Quay. I arrived at the normally heaving Lounge at about eleven on a Saturday evening. I wanted to show my friend the trendy side of Phnom Penh's bar scene and share a drink on one of the balconies overlooking the Tonle Sap River. My ex-Reuters colleague was only in town for a few days. I took her to the Lounge so she could mingle with some of the city's twenty-something revellers and strut her stuff on the club's lively dance floor.

As we arrived at the Lounge on the corner of Sisowath Quay, I spotted a silver Hummer parked on the pavement near the door. I also noticed a stream of lively young Khmer party-goers descending the narrow steps from the club upstairs. As we ascended and arrived on the first floor near the bar, I thought nothing more of it. The place was empty.

"That's odd," I remarked. "This place is usually packed."

As I stepped up to the bar, I was approached by a handsome young Khmer man and his female companion with model-like looks. He placed an entire bottle of whisky on the bar top and slapped me on the back.

"Drink with me!"

I knew that refusing to drink with someone was rude in Khmer culture. I knocked back three whiskies in the space of ten minutes.

"I think you had better go," I said to my guest. "This looks like it could get ugly."

And it did. My guest returned to her hotel, and I stayed drinking with the Khmer man and his girlfriend. It turned out that he was the son of another Oknha. He also had a reputation for pulling out guns in nightclubs and shooting them at passersby - just for the hell of it.

As for me, I had little recollection of what happened that night, but I know that when I returned to the Lounge some days later, the French nightclub manager, Serge, reprimanded me.

"Are you crazy!?! He broke my bar!" Serge cried, pointing to a crack in the six-inch deep wooden slab that was the bar top. "He broke my bar!"

"Oh!" was all I could think to say. "Sorry about that."

I couldn't remember anything. Perhaps Miss Bopha was right in her suspicion that Phnom Penh could be a dangerous place after dark. I was lucky my drinking buddy hadn't broken my head, by all accounts.

TARAS

HAVING PUT the TV channel on air and having had my fill of Cambodia's "business development,' I needed a break. I decided to go home to England. I informed Bradley and booked my trip. I also wanted to consider my own future too. Part of me wanted to return to journalism.

When it came time to leave, I patted Showkie on the head, gave Seila a couple of hundred dollars to tide him over and said fond farewells to Miss Bopha. I took a Thai Airways flight to London.

The last time I had been in England was three years ago, and as we entered the terminal building, I was somewhat startled by what I saw. For a start, it was cleaner than what I was used to. The people were also taller, stouter, and fully clothed in jackets, suits, sweaters, and scarves. It took some getting used to. After all, now I was more used to dusty immigration halls with petite Asians attired in silk wraps and embroidered tops.

Having passed through the immigration formalities and

collected my luggage, I headed for a line of black cabs for the journey into London. I was headed for my flat in Fulham.

It was April, and most of my journalist friends were on assignment in Iraq covering the second Gulf War, which had started in March. Many were embedded with British and American troops.

When I arrived home at my flat in Fulham, I first turned on the television. I couldn't help but notice that all the old faces still dominated the airwaves – especially morning talk shows.

Having missed the early morning news programs, I flipped over to the BBC's text-based news service Ceefax and quickly glanced at the news headlines.

One headline, in particular, stood out. It concerned the death of journalists at the Palestine Hotel in Baghdad. The first reports were sketchy and scant in detail. They did not say who or what organisations the journalists worked for. The report actually raised more questions than it answered. It made me feel uneasy.

Disturbed, I left my flat and wandered down Fulham Road toward Putney Bridge. It was still early, and some shops were just starting to open up. I was headed to a camping shop in Parsons Green. I needed new walking shoes that would withstand dusty, pot-holed Phnom Penh pavements and thoroughfares.

As I peered in the window, I received an overseas call. The name did not register, but I recognised it as a Singapore number.

"Hi mate..." the caller started. "Sorry, but..."

It was the head of Reuters Television's bureau in Asia.

"I know Jules...I know," I replied, trying to make it easier for him to deliver the news. "Who is it?"

"I am really sorry to have to tell you ...but it is Taras."

Taras and I had worked together in Kosovo on several occasions. We had covered Kosovo before NATO bombed Belgrade in 1999. We also covered the NATO-led KFOR mission that was put in place to ensure security on the ground in Kosovo after the bombing campaign ended. In both cases, we were based in Pristina.

On our first tour, Taras and I covered the Kosovo Albanians' anti-Serbian demonstrations as they brought the Kosovan capital Pristina to a standstill. On one occasion, I was forced to leave Taras filming and head off to a satellite feed point with our coverage to meet a deadline. When I returned, things had taken a turn for the worse. A group of Serbian thugs set upon some straggling Kosovo Albanian demonstrators. Taras was still filming.

Just as I arrived, Taras was set upon by the very same group of black leather-jacketed Serb thugs that I had seen from a distance. They grabbed his camera and smashed it on the ground. By the time I arrived, it was broken in two. I reached in and pulled him out.

March 19

At least two television cameramen working for Western
news agencies were beaten by plainclothes policemen
while attempting to film mass demonstrations in Pristina.
Taras Protsyuk, a Ukrainian camera operator working for
Reuters TV, was attacked as he shot footage of a weeping
Albanian woman who said she was struck by police
during a rally. Protsyuk fell to the ground and his video

camera was smashed. The assailants repeatedly punched him in the face until his producer, Glen Felgate, managed to pull him away. He suffered minor injuries.

Although Taras was Ukrainian, he was based in Warsaw, Poland. He was a mainstay of the Reuters Television operation in Russia and Eastern Europe. He had covered Chechnya and many other conflicts on numerous occasions. He had a great attitude and a ready smile – no matter the situation. He was a sheer joy to know and work with.

"Damn it! I knew it was someone I knew. I saw the report on Ceefax. I just knew it! Thanks for telling me, Jules. Thanks."

And that was how I began my holiday in England. I spent the rest of the day wandering in a daze, cutting my holiday short. I was haunted by Taras' death. After all, as a journalist, he was just one of several colleagues and friends killed in the line of fire.

Taras brought back some harsh memories of my previous life when I was traipsing the world's warzones for Reuters.

As a journalist with Reuters, I had covered wars in Bosnia, Kosovo, Africa and the Middle East.

I had left Sierra Leone with two coffins. Inside those coffins were the corpses of two of my best friends. During my ten-year career with Reuters, I was shot at on Sarajevo's infamous Sniper Alley more times than I care to remember, blown up in a TV building in the Bosnian capital just days before my 32nd birthday, assaulted by secret police in Albania while covering the collapse of government-backed pyramid schemes, and unceremoniously dumped on the banks of the Congo River in Kinshasa - with tens of thousands of dollars strapped to my person. I had escaped the first Gulf War but had been to Iraq several times in my career. I had filmed Saddam Hussein's son Uday, and interviewed world leaders at the World Economic Forum in Davos. Among those I had doorstepped or interviewed were Yasser Arafat, Kofi Annan, Prince Albert of Monaco, Benjamin Netanyahu and Thabo Mbeki.

For a brief moment, I hankered to do all that again. I was considering returning to journalism and the cut and thrust of covering wars and politics, and policy. But then Taras' death put my life back into perspective. Did I really want to dodge bullets and shells and question the powers that be?

The answer was no.

Despite the trials and tribulations of putting a TV channel to air in Cambodia, I decided I was right where I wanted to be. Warzones were no longer for me – Oknha and the TV channel were. I just hoped that the friends I had lost with Reuters along the way would concur that my new vocation of teaching Cambodians how to do TV was worthwhile. I certainly thought so - for the time being, anyway.

NOT ENOUGH COCK, SIR!

WHEN I RETURNED TO CAMBODIA, the studio was almost ready. We planned a grand opening. The cock-fighting Deputy Prime Minister would open it. He arrived in regal attire, gave a speech and watched a medley of performances in the sound-proofed sound stage. Our studio was officially open, and Oknha was happy – head office grinned and bore it.

We could do local and international concerts and events with the newly opened studio – just as Oknha had envisioned. And it was with some bewilderment that I received an email one day from our floor manager Bora entitled NOT ENOUGH COCK SIR!

Dear Sir,
I like to report that audience in group getting restless. The
reason for this is that they are not getting enough cock.
I would like to report that advertising agency and
marketing company give the audience a lot of cock. That

makes audience happy. I think should give our audience something.
Best Regards,
Bora

Having been in-country for some time now, I found that I could actually decipher this email with little effort. Bora was trying to tell me in his own inimitable way that other companies that held concerts gave the audience free Coca-Cola and that we should do the same.

After intensive discussions with our small but growing team, we went a step further than our competitors. We elected to offer our audience energy drinks. We stopped short of handing out Viagra!

As well as local concerts, we also started bringing in international artists.

"Can we bring J-Lo?" Oknha asked excitedly at one of our weekly meetings.

"Have you got a million dollars?" I replied.

"Mmmmmmm, Mmmmm, Mmmmm," came the reply.

Instead, we settled on Michael Learns to Rock or MLTR.

Michael Learns to Rock were not particularly famous in their native Denmark and Europe. They were huge in Asia. They were also huge in Cambodia – courtesy of the fact that their hits had been ripped off and re-recorded by Khmer recording artists. Those artists mysteriously went very quiet as the date for the concert neared. However, the buzz around town was palpable – thanks to our channel's marketing efforts.

MLTR sounded a lot like Westlife. In fact, if you heard their songs, you would think that they were Westlife. Made famous throughout Asia for their rendition of the song Take Me to Your Heart and fronted by blonde-haired Jascha Richter, MLTR – as they had become known – originally consisted of four band members. By the time they came to Cambodia, there were officially three of them. Their hit songs included You Took My Heart Away, That's Why (You Go Away), Sleeping Child and 25 Minutes.

"We're bringing Michael Learns to Rock," I informed one of my advertising agency friends after I had done the deal with promoter Michael Hosking of Midas Promotions.

"Wow, they're huge," he replied immediately. "What a great choice."

At a time when no international bands came to Phnom Penh, it was quite a radical initiative to try and bring anyone at all. I was also determined that Michael Learns to Rock and the promoter would see that we could pull an international concert off so that others would want to come. I paid particular attention to the technical rider.

"We need Carlsberg beer," I informed Bora, our floor manager.

"No have, sir," came the reply. "Have Angkor."

"No, it clearly says Carlsberg," I went on. "They must be chilled and placed in the fridge when they come off stage."

"Cambodia no has Carlsburrr," Bora replied firmly, dropping the 'g' in the process.

I called Mr. Bunthoeun.

"We need Carlsberg beer," I explained to Bunthoeun in the hope that, as Oknha's designated drinker, he would know where to find it.

"Can't they drink Angkor?" came the reply.

"Apparently, not."

"I'll fix it," Mr. Bunthoeun responded cheerfully. "Leave it to me."

With the Carlsberg situation being taken care of, I then started planning the actual concert.

The concert itself was going to be kept small. It would effectively be a studio concert with ticket giveaways. We were expecting an audience of about one thousand which was small compared to the tens of thousands of fans that Michael Learns to Rock was ordinarily used to. The promoter called it a 'studio concert'.

As the marketing ratcheted up, so did the interest. Requests were coming in from advertisers and dignitaries alike. Oknha also got in on the act, suggesting I write a letter to the prime minister's office to see if he would like to meet the band members. The reply was, 'Unfortunately, the prime minister was out of town on that particular day', so the deputy prime minister was called in to service the request'. It was the 'cock-fighting deputy prime minister' once again.

There were also charity visits to arrange and a little bit of sightseeing. The band had opted to spend the night before the concert in a local bar. They would spend the morning after the show at Cambodia's Tuol Sleng genocide museum. There would also be press conferences and photo-ops in between.

"What about piracy?" came the inevitable question at the press conference on the morning of the event.

"We are aware of it, and we don't condone it," the band's drummer Kare Wanscher explained. He was the best person to field that question because he was qualified as a lawyer.

After the press conference, I took the band on a tour of Phnom Penh. They loved the ambience and the 'look-and-feel' of the place. They also loved that they were not mobbed by fans and autograph hunters.

"Cambodians are shy," I explained to the lead singer Jascha over a beer the night before the concert. "They may not even clap after your songs. They may just sit there in silence. Don't be offended. They will still like it."

"Don't worry. It'll be a good concert," Jascha reassured me.

On event day, I arrived at the studio a few hours before the event to check on crowd control and ticketing. As I stepped from my car, I glanced at the sky to check the weather. It was now the rainy season, and the usually clear blue sky had become mottled with grey as rain clouds gathered overhead. It looked like rain, and I panicked momentarily, thinking that people might not venture out. After all, many of our ticket-winners were youngsters who used *motos* as their primary means of transport. Sometimes they preferred to avoid navigating flooded and pot-holed roads.

However, I needn't have worried. An hour before doors opened, many people were already snaking along the road outside. Some of those at the front were pushing up against our metal-grilled gates, peering longingly through at us as we talked. It had not gotten to the point where people at the back pushed those in front, desperately attempting to move things along. But I was sure that would happen soon.

"Let's open up in twenty minutes," I told Bora.

And with that, I took one last look at the MLTR fans.

They ranged in age from five years old to fifty. There was no doubt that MLTR was popular – in Cambodia as in Asia.

Once inside the studio, the concertgoers politely jockeyed for position. Most wanted to see their international idols in person, as close to the stage as possible. The atmosphere had become electric, and ushers stood patiently in the wings, watching the crowd. The lighting technicians swivelled the moving heads sending arcs of red, green and blue lights careering off the stage, the walls and the curtains. The venue had an air of anticipation as if something big was about to happen. I hoped our show would live up to the expectation and hype.

Backstage I bumped into the band. They were relaxed as they sat patiently waiting in the changing rooms. It was then that their manager came up to me.

"Is this a joke," the moustachioed Swedish manager asked as he held out a bath towel.

"Sorry?" I replied.

"These towels? Is this a joke?" he asked again. "They are too big."

I looked puzzled.

"It's in the rider," he added sternly. "You must follow the rider."

"Can we cut them in half?" I asked desperately.

The manager paused, twiddled his moustache and sighed.

"That will work," he said at last.

And with that, the show went on.

My relief was short-lived. No sooner had the show started when I started receiving text messages. So did Mr. Bunthoeun. Oknha had assigned Mr. Buntheoun to help me with the protocol arrangements for the band and to introduce me to the deputy prime minister.

"This is bull$%#!" one message read.

"Is this a joke?" cried another.

"Where's the sound, *#^&head?"

Mr. Bunthoeun was getting similar messages from his Khmer contacts.

"What the hell's going on!?!" I yelled at Mr. Bunthoeun over Jascha belting out MLTR's hit Paint My Love.

Bunthoeun pointed at the TV set in our reception and made a sweeping gesture at his throat. I could see the band on stage with flashing lights and dry ice rising from the stage. They continued to belt out their hits as I turned up the volume on the TV set.

Mute.

I couldn't believe it. We had pumped the concert so much that people who couldn't get tickets were sitting in bars, cafes and at home in anticipation of this historic performance by the first international band to play in Cambodia for years.

"Oh," Mr. Buntheoun groaned. "It's the deputy prime minister's office. His protocol says he is embarrassed. They're asking what's happening?"

"Tell them we're fixing it," I cried desperately.

I made frantic calls to our network control room at the broadcast centre thirty minutes away.

"Decoder not work, sir!" our Head of Engineering, Sothea, told me.

"Fix it! Please fix it!"

As it happened, it took Sothea and his team about 45 minutes to fix the sound on the TV. During that time, Mr.

Bunthoeun and I were bombarded with hundreds of expletives in English and Khmer. In the end, I turned my phone off. Mr. Bunthoeun couldn't, just in case the government called him. After all, the band had met the deputy prime minister just that afternoon.

Despite the on-air glitch, the concert went off without a hitch. The sound in the studio was perfect, and Jascha belted out his biggest hits while interacting with the audience.

What had actually happened was that the link between the studio and our broadcast was broken. It meant that the control room could receive pictures but no sound. Ordinarily, our team could have fixed the technical problem by merely rebooting the decoder. This time they panicked. The occasion was just too big for them. They froze.

The sound came good halfway through the band's set. We replayed the concert with sound to appease an already angered TV audience. After the show, the band sat in the dressing room sipping Carlsberg beer, watching their performance.

"It looks great," Jascha said.

"How are you enjoying those beers?" I asked, quickly changing the subject.

"They're great," the band members replied in unison.

"I should hope so. We flew them in from Malaysia," one of them replied.

"Why did you do that?"

"It says Carlsberg in the technical rider."

"Nobody reads those things..." someone replied.

I kept mum about the fact that we had broadcast their first-ever Cambodia concert without sound.

DESPITE THE ODD HICCUP, our channel steadily rose in the rankings. We held onto our number one position with ever-innovative concerts, reality shows, and format game shows and sporting events. We had about 70% of the country's television viewership. Even the head office was impressed - and surprised. Oknha asked for a second channel. And, after some pretty fast talking by both Oknha and myself, he got one.

"Glen is turning business away," Oknha told head office. "We need a new channel."

It was actually true and not just a ruse to fill Cambodia's airwaves and extend Oknha's reach even more. We had become so popular with advertisers that we were running 30-minute programs to 30-minute commercials, which was unsustainable for any TV channel worldwide.

To alleviate the commercial pressure, I put our advertising rates up mid-year. This was unheard of in Cambodian culture, and the sales team couldn't handle it. I had to look at every booking in minute detail before signing advertising contracts – and some contracts I turned down. I refused to take certain bookings. This was unheard of, and the sales department, whose idea of selling commercials was to continue dropping the price until a sale was realised, resigned. They hated that they now had to say 'no' to their corporate friends making the bookings.

So, having heard that we were turning business away, the head office relented. Oknha would get a second channel with a budget even tighter than the first.

"No buildings, no infrastructure. You know the score! No More studios!" was the refrain from the head office.

I then set about creating a concept for yet another TV Channel. I came up with an idea for a youth channel with the ever-popular K-Pop music in mind. It was aimed at the 'NOW' generation. There would be music videos, idol dramas, music downloads, and a corresponding website. It would unite Cambodia's youth with the rest of Asia. It was intended to be interactive and help the mobile phone company offer value-added services.

"We'll need a studio," I informed Bradley. "But it will be a small one."

"Oh, no," Bradley replied, knowing full well that the new channel would stall and that he and I would be stuck between Oknha and the head office.

"We'll build it anyway," somebody said.

And we did. We engaged an Australian contractor and started making plans. It was a low-rise building with a control room, a small three-person studio, and office space. It would take about nine months to build – under ordinary circumstances.

However, unfortunately, circumstances were far from ordinary. The head office then developed the nasty habit of sending auditors in. And since those particular auditors had no inkling that we were building another studio, we had to keep the whole project under wraps.

"Mate, down tools, get the workmen off-site and shut the gates," I would order the ocker-Aussie foreman when I got wind of yet another visit from the head office.

"Mate, it's going to delay completion," he moaned.

"No choice, mate. Please just do it," I begged. The Aussie contractor relented. He would kick everyone off-site and close the sheet metal gates. The building would temporarily disappear, and head office was none-the-wiser.

"God, that was close," I would sigh to Bradley when the auditors left the studio complex, having been within 100 yards of our new building. "Anyway, I'll get the builders back."

With the studio's construction continuing, we continued to do deals with record labels and producers of Korean idol dramas. We then sought presenters.

With vivid memories of receiving thousands of CVs and applications the last time I looked for staff sometime before, I didn't advertise in local newspapers this time around. Instead, we used websites and our own existing TV channels to ask wannabe celebs to send clips of themselves to us via email and text. This time we received a much more manageable five hundred applications.

"He looks Korean," one of our producers said.

"Then let's hire him," I replied enthusiastically.

"...a bit too Korean for Cambodia."

"Oh."

"This one looks half-Cambodian, half-Korean, though."

"OK, let's hire him then."

"What about her? Her name is Julie."

"Looks Chinese but has an English name," I remarked.

"Chinese is OK. English names are trendy," I was told.

"OK."

Screen testing presenters for the 'NOW' generation was hard work. After about a week of sifting through clips and CVs, we had five young, trendy recent college graduates as the country's first-ever VJs.

With the VJs now in place, we set about filming programs, promos, and channel idents. With a month to go before our launch, it was all going to plan. And then, one of my producers bounded into my office sweating profusely and out of breath.

"We have a problem with Julie, our VJ."

"Julie? What happened?" I asked, thinking our attractive female presenter was embroiled in a scandal of some kind.

"She leaving us, sir!"

"Leaving!?! She is one of our main presenters! She is in almost all of our programs! And we haven't even started yet."

"Yes, sir! Parent no like! They saw test transmission. They saw Julie wearing makeup."

"What do you mean 'no like'?"

"You put Julie program on TV, and now her parents are embarrassed and keep her in the house!"

"But she's our presenter. She signed a contract!"

"Parent no care! They rich Cambodian-Chinese family. Julie on TV is embarrassing. They know stars have affair with general and minister. This big loss of face for Julie family. They no allow!"

"Maybe I should speak to Oknha?"

"No need. I already contact. He say forget it. Move on. He knows the family. He knows they will not change."

"In Cambodia, star not like in your country," Bora continued. "In Cambodia star have affair with general or minister or businessman. In Cambodia star have not so good reputation. Many parents don't want children to be star or on TV."

Moving on was more challenging than it sounded. Julie had been a mainstay of our new channel's programming. She appeared in programs alongside our trendy Korean-looking male presenters. She also appeared in the channel promos and idents – the fillers that ran between programs.

"We'll replace her with a cartoon," I announced.

"Sir?" Bora replied, looking at me sympathetically, thinking I had lost the plot.

"We will superimpose a cartoon over her but keep her voice," I tried again.

"Can! Can!" Bora shouted excitedly. "That's why you head of TV channel, boss! You have a good idea, sir!."

And with that, Cambodia's first ever youth channel went on air with bizarre-looking MTV-style music programmes fronted by trendy Korean-looking Cambodian hosts and a somewhat questionable 'Who Framed Roger Rabbit'-style cartoon character of a Khmer girl named Julie. The cartoon character's mouth moved up and down like a goldfish's vaguely in time to her speech. We kept

Julie's actual recorded speech. It worked – for a while, anyway.

The youth were starting to take to the channel. They were downloading songs on their mobile phones, sending us music video requests and sending in their own playlists by text message and email. However, I felt something was missing.

"Can the youngsters' text messages appear on screen?" I asked Sothea.

"Can!" came the enthusiastic reply from our head of engineering.

"Well, let's try it!" I exclaimed excitedly.

We launched the new text-to-TV gimmick, and within an hour, we were getting 1000 texts an hour. I patted myself on the back.

Just as I was revelling in our success, our head of news, Mr. Som, bounded into the room, wiping sweat from his brow with a checked handkerchief. He looked flustered.

"Il y a un problem," Mr. Som addressed me in French. Being an elder Khmer, he spoke fluent French. He had attended the local lycee before the Khmer Rouge took power. At that time, Cambodia had been a French protectorate, and many elites learned French instead of English. He also had close ties to the Prime Minister, whose policies he sympathised with immensely.

"They say PM f*#K off!"

"F*#k off!" I repeated, appalled.

"Oui! They say CPP F*#k off, too!," Mr. Som continued referring to the prime minister's ruling party. "Oknha not happy!"

"Oh!"

I picked up the phone to Sothea. "Mr. Sothea, please stop the texts!"

"But we just started! Many people send message," Sothea replied proudly. "Work very well. Audience happy!"

"Yes. Wrong messages! Tell PM F*#k off!"

There was silence at the end of the phone for a few seconds. And then I heard Sothea bellowing at his staff in panic.

"Message stop! Message stop!" Sothea exclaimed.

I watched as the text message bar at the bottom of the screen in front of me disappeared. Mr. Som slumped into an armchair opposite my desk.

"On a besoin a censurer," Mr. Som sighed.

"Yes, we need a censor," I agreed. "Can you arrange it?"

"Biensur," Mr. Som nodded happily.

As it happened, Mr. Som hired an army of censors whose sole job was to ensure that no swear words appeared on screen – and, more importantly, no foul language aimed at the prime minister or his political party.

The one thousand texts per hour continued – most of them were song requests and greetings to VJs, friends, and relatives. They even created their own language. It had become the country's unique Facebook messenger – even before Facebook existed in Cambodia.

Bradley, Oknha and the head office were happy. They called it synergy.

DON'T BRING ME A PROBLEM

HAVING LAUNCHED two channels now in Cambodia, I experienced a period of calm - both at work and at play. The TV channels were maintaining their top rankings, and Miss Bopha was going about her business contentedly and, at times, quietly.

To capitalise on the TV channels' success, I looked at ways to diversify and build upon what we had created. After all, we had stars and music and platforms to promote and sell them on TV. I tabled a proposition to create our own record label. I presented the plan to Oknha and Bradley at one of our regular weekly meetings.

"We can build up a stable of stars," I started. "We have the platform with TV. All we need is the product. We can create singers. I only need the songs. I can get from publishers and producers in Thailand and localise."

"It is a great idea," Bradley chimed in. "We can offer up more downloads and ringtones as part of our value-added services for mobile phones."

"Hmmm, hmmm, hmmm", Oknha replied as he stared out of the Cambodiana's top-floor window at the majestically moving Tonle Sap as the grey-brown waters merged with the Mekong. I followed Oknha's gaze. In the distance, I could see wooden long-tail fishing boats drifting laconically on the river's shimmering surface. It was a peaceful, serene scene.

"My relative is also starting a record label," Oknha began. "That means you will be in competition with him. That could be difficult. You don't know my relative."

I looked at Bradley, and he looked at me. We knew some of Okhna's relatives. Some could be quite difficult.

"I like your idea. But please don't bring me a problem with my family," Oknha added, effectively stopping the conversation.

I put the new idea for a record label out of my mind and concentrated on running the TV channels.

It was business as usual, and I would meet Bradley for a beer a few times a week. Our bar of choice was The Gym.

"Where are you?" Oknha announced one night in his customary greeting to Bradley. "We're having a family gathering. Come along. Bring Glen."

Knocking back our respective beers, Bradley and I jumped in our cars and headed toward Oknha's sister's house.

As we turned off Norodom Boulevard onto one of the

side-streets military police stood at strategic points in the road. They sat watching the comings and goings of passers-by with their AK-47 rifles resting on their knees or slung casually over their shoulders. As we approached Oknha's sister's house, I spotted a white Bentley, an assortment of Land Cruisers and an ornate-looking golf cart parked outside the street. Uniformed drivers traded high-pitched banter as they stood near their respective vehicles, ever ready for their partying bosses' return.

Approaching the gate, a uniformed security guard stepped from a smart-looking guard hut and smiled at us. He was dressed head to toe in military attire.

"Please," the guard said, displaying a row of crooked teeth. "Oknha is waiting."

"Ahhh, Bradley....Glen....., come, join us," Oknha turned to us as we walked in. "You know everyone here."

There then followed a bout of Cambodian-style drinking. I, for one, was utterly plastered.

"Let's go to the club," Mr. Bunthoeun announced excitedly. The club Mr. Bunthoeun referred to belonged to one of Oknha's relatives.

Within fifteen minutes, I was strutting along a red carpet at the glass-fronted entrance of a nightclub. We strolled up a massive marble-stepped staircase leading to a red-carpeted landing that gave onto two narrow corridors. Mr. Bunthoeun and I took the one on the left and walked to the end of the corridor past door upon door of rooms with placards announcing EXECUTIVE SUITE. There were six of them. Ultimately, we stopped in front of a door with a placard saying VVIP SUITE.

The door swung open to reveal a dark cavernous interior with subdued red lighting placed strategically along the walls. In the middle of the room sat one of Oknha's relatives. He was the club's owner.

"Please, have a whisky."

"Champay!" Oknha's relative said as he lifted his full whisky glass to his lips and motioned for me to do the same. He then poured another round.

"Champay!" Oknha's relative called again. We emptied our glasses again. And then again. By the third, I bowed politely and declined.

"You must drink!" Oknha's relative ordered.

I did as I was told once again. By this time, the room was spinning, and my speech was slurred.

"Champay!" Oknha's relative called again as he poured another two fingers of the amber liquid into my glass.

"Really...I can't."

"Drink!"

"Look, I cannot drink anymore," I slurred.

Oknha's relative then became aggressive.

"Drink!" he spat, pouring even more whisky into my glass.

"Look!" I countered. "I don't answer to you! I answer to Oknha and Bradley and head office. I don't have to drink or champay or do anything."

I looked across to see Mr. Bunthoeun staring at me in bewilderment.

Then, I noticed Oknha's relative signalling to the armed, uniformed men who stood around the room. Two stepped forward, hoisted me off my barstool, and dragged me to the door. My toes dragged along the ground as they manhandled me out of the room.

By this time, I had lost control of my legs and almost every other faculty. But there again, I didn't need them – the bodyguards were doing most of the work. The last thing I remember was Oknha's relative barking into a phone while glaring at me as I made my ungainly departure.

"Glen has disrespected me..." I heard the relative say.

The following day, I woke up in a blind panic. I had no idea where I was or how I got there. The night before was a complete blank. I opened my eyes to a darkened room that I didn't recognise. I opened the curtains to reveal a massive picture window looking onto the Tonle Sap River. Directly below my room, there was a swimming pool. I saw the Hotel Cambodiana insignia emblazoned across one of the swimming pool umbrellas. My heart sank as the events of the night before came flooding back.

Within a few hours, I was seated across from Oknha.

"I told you, don't bring me a problem with my family. And that's exactly what you've done!" Oknha said.

"You should have known better than to take him there in his drunken state," Oknha then said to Mr. Bunthoeun in Khmer. "What on earth were you thinking?"

"Oknha, please don't blame Mr. Bunthoeun... I'm responsible for my own actions," I said timidly. "I'm sorry I caused you this problem. I was stupid."

"Fix it! Just fix it! Fix it - or else!"

As it happened, 'fixing it' proved easier said than done. Oknha's relative wouldn't accept my apology.

Even Miss Bopha got worried when she heard of the trouble that I was in. A few days later, she appeared in the driveway with an orange-robed monk with a shiny bald head. She said something in Khmer to the monk and made me kneel on the front patio facing the monk with my palms clasped together. She forced my head gently downwards so that my head was lower than that of our guest, who had taken up a cross-legged position opposite me. The monk placed a bowl of water at his side, and on closer inspection, I noticed that pink flower petals and white lotus buds were floating on top of the crystal-clear water. The monk smiled at me and then started chanting. As he did so, he dipped a sheaf made from what looked like leaves into the bowl and flicked them at me, thus dousing me from head to torso with scented water.

This went on for about thirty minutes, by which time my shirt was soaked entirely, and streams of water were running down my forehead onto my face and neck. The chanting stopped, and the monk once again smiled at me.

"Now bad luck and bad spirit is gone," Miss Bopha announced after the monk had departed. "Now your problems will go too. Oknha will leave you alone."

It didn't fix my problem in the slightest, despite the best efforts of Mr. Bunthoeun and a few others on my staff who desperately tried to get Oknha's relative to accept my apology for disrespecting him. All the dousing had done was give me a cold.

It took a year for Oknha's relative to accept my apology.

He did so when we were at another party. He grabbed a whisky bottle from a nearby table and smiled.

"Glen, I am going to teach you how to drink!" Oknha's relative announced.

He drank me under the table once again - but this time I made sure to keep my mouth shut.

Having made my peace with Oknha's relative, I did a lot of soul-searching in the days and weeks after. It all came down to whether I wanted to be a big fish in a small pond or a small fish in a big pond. And the reason was that my old employer Reuters had offered me the Beijing TV bureau. It meant that I would be in charge of covering the Beijing Olympics. It was a plum position. It merited serious consideration.

To help my decision and clear my head, I took off to Bamboo Island, a few miles off the country's south coast. The only way to get there was by boat.

"You're in charge," I said to Bora as I climbed into my four-wheel drive, pointed my car south and headed off on a three-hour drive to Sihanoukville.

En route, I gazed out the window at the farmland, garment factories, and occasional pagoda. Huts on stilts littered the landscape, and as I peered closer, I could see cows tethered to the houses' stilts standing next to massive clay jars laden with water and grain. I marvelled at the simplicity of the existence on display before me. I wondered if the owners of those houses and cows and water jugs were actually happy with their lot. After all, theirs' was an existence reliant upon the land and devoid of the rest of the world's modern-day trappings. Do they even have a TV?

"Because we have the number one TV channel, the Prime Minister loves me," Oknha had once said to Bradley and me during one of our regular weekly meetings. At the time, I wondered if Oknha was thanking us, encouraging us, or boasting. Perhaps all three, I determined later.

As I drove, I pondered my lot and how I got here. I started out in TV in broadcast journalism. It was a field that was deadly serious. In fact, it was deathly. I had lost friends and colleagues along the way.

There had been the Bosnian war where in June 1995, I had been blown up in the local TV building with other colleagues. The Bosnian Serb rocket had landed in the TV building's atrium blowing out windows and destroying the building's basement. Dozens of people were injured, including my good friend Faridoun, who almost lost his eye, and Hanna, whose pretty face was peppered with glass splinters. I had escaped unscathed but had ferried some of those injured to hospital.

And then there was Kosovo, where in 1998, I had come to the aid of my good friend Taras as he was jumped on by Serbian thugs who had smashed his camera in two – and then tried to do the same to his face. I had waded in and managed to drag him from the melee. Again, I was unscathed but shaken. Taras, of course, had been killed years later during the US-led invasion of Iraq.

There was also Kinshasa and Brazzaville, and finally, Sierra Leone. On my second trip to Freetown, I lost my good friends Kurt Schork, and Miguel Gil Moreno in an ambush thought to be carried out by the Revolutionary United Front (RUF) child soldiers. I had touched down at Sierra Leone's Lunghi airport just 24 hours before the fatal attack and then dealt with the aftermath. I left with the bodies to attend funerals and memorial services in Spain and the United States.

I pondered my checkered past as I hopped on the long-tail boat bound for Bamboo Island. We bounced across the blue-green ocean with frothy white caps breaking against our boat. Within half an hour, the blindingly white sand of Bamboo Island came into view – as did the bamboo huts and a thatch-roofed restaurant. I hopped into the surf, hoisted my backpack over the bow and trudged up to the bar-cum-reception.

"Enjoy, sir," the T-shirt-clad Khmer receptionist said as he checked me in and pointed down the beach. "Your hut number 6."

Hut number 6 was much like the other huts that lined the beach. Constructed entirely of wood. Rickety steps led to the small balcony and the flimsy front door, which was locked with a padlock. Inside everything was dark. There was no electricity; the only concession to light was a torch dangling from a hook on the wall. With the light from the open door creeping into the bungalow, I could make out the wooden bed with a simple mattress and sheet. There was no wash basin or toilet in the room. They were in the outhouse just behind the huts at the beach's edge as it disappeared into the palm fronds behind.

Depositing my backpack on the bed, I pulled out a towel and made for the beach. I threw it on the sand and headed for the surf. Unlike Thai beaches I had been to, Bamboo Island had surf. Blue-grey waves crashed upon the sand. I strolled into the water's edge and marvelled at the quality of the soft sand as it squelched between my toes. I immersed myself in the sea.

After my dip, I strolled to the bar and bought a beer.

"No food in the room, sir. Have rat," the receptionist-cum-bartender informed me.

"No problem, I'll eat here," I politely replied. "See you this evening."

I then took my beer and returned to my bungalow, where I crawled into the hammock on my balcony. I sipped my beer, closed my eyes and listened to the ocean. Once again, I considered my position.

When I arrived in Cambodia over a year ago, I found a city battered and bruised. It was a city struggling to lift itself to its feet. Step by faltering step, the country was desperately trying to find its foothold in a world that – in the face of the Khmer Rouge - had turned its back so unashamedly on the Cambodian people some thirty-five years before.

But despite the international community's past betrayals, I found people who were warm and welcoming and willing to laugh at themselves and their inadequacies. They were also hungry to learn and desperate to get ahead. After all, they knew that they had been left behind. They accepted that their situation had mainly been brought about by their own making. They longed for the day that they could take their rightful place in Southeast Asia, Asia, and the world.

The Cambodians wanted to emulate their neighbours.

They wanted gleaming skyscrapers, traffic-clad motorways, and a thriving airport. They wanted all the trappings of a modern-day South East Asian success story. They wanted to join the economic development party. And above all, they wanted to make their presence felt. Within a very short time, I became sympathetic to their cause. I wanted to help.

"If I come to Cambodia will I be safe?" a Singaporean once asked me gingerly when I spoke of Phnom Penh.

"Of course," I replied confidently. "You are as safe as you would be in New York, London, or anywhere else – unless you do something silly. In fact, you're actually safer."

And then he, like other would-be visitors, arranged his meetings, booked his flights and then showed up at Pochentong Airport – apprehensively at first. In town for just a few days, I took my guest to the Foreign Correspondent's Club overlooking the Tonle Sap River, a French colonial restaurant and a local bar. He loved the ambience, the architecture and the people. He was entranced. He wouldn't be the last – by a long stretch.

"When can we meet again?" the Singaporean asked longingly. "I'll come and see you."

So, despite my colleagues' inferiority complex and insecurity, Phnom Penh had a certain allure. Even though in 2002 Cambodia – to me at least - was Africa in Asia, it had a certain charm, a certain grace that had long since been scrubbed from other Asian capitals by populations eager to modernise and live in apartments and work in tower blocks and drive along expressways. In Cambodia, there were still tree-clad boulevards and two- and three-story shophouses interspersed with French colonial villas, breezy verandas, and quaint wooden shutters sealing out the sun from first-floor bedrooms with ceiling fans whirring laconically in the darkened rooms.

There were also dusty boulder-strewn side streets, pot-holed boulevards, pockmarked pavements, and decayed and decrepit buildings side-by-side with colourful, chaotic markets teeming with life. Houses, shops and schools were barely standing. Cars and trucks were barely moving. All about them was the detritus of war, the detritus of a country left to the evil devices of the Khmer Rouge. Was it any wonder that my Khmer friends and colleagues were insecure about themselves, their country, and their home?

Despite all of their misgivings, the people smiled. They smiled through their hardship, poverty, and unfortunate lot in life. They smiled at the sun as it beat fiercely upon their skin and the rain as it pelted their heads. They smiled and smiled and smiled. Here were a people that would endure no matter what. Here were people who were stubbornly resilient and fiercely proud – and so they should be for what they had survived.

And for this, I respected them. I admired the fact that this was a people that, no matter what they endured, they would never give up. I also admired the fact that even with the most meagre resources, these Khmers would often succeed – not always, but often. And if they didn't, they would find another way. In Cambodia, there was always a way.

In addition to being determined, resilient, and hardy, they were loyal, fun-loving, and decent. They held on to family values that had long ceased to exist in the West. They disciplined their children in a tender, loving manner. They ensured that they grew up with the same family values that they, as parents, had also learned. They respected one another and did as much as possible to avoid confrontation. After all, there had been enough confrontation, enough heartbreak in their recent past.

And while the Cambodians were busy getting on with the heady challenges of attempting to 'normalise' their country and improve their lot, the world at large would always appear to know better. It was as if the world had put Cambodia in a box and stuck a label on it, which read 'Basket Case'. It was as if the world had written Cambodia off. And there were those, it seemed, that didn't want the country to change, to develop, to take its rightful place amongst its Southeast Asian neighbours. Some wanted Cambodia to stay right where it was – a downtrodden disability on the anatomy of Asia. This was evidenced by the stories and the headlines that appeared week after week in the foreign media.

And when I thought of the news stories about Cambodia, I thought of my past life as a journalist. I thought of my former colleagues who had stuck with me through thick and thin in wars in Bosnia and Kosovo and in the Congos and Sierra Leone and in allied bombing runs in Iraq and natural disasters in Mozambique.

And although I hadn't spoken much about my past life for many years, it all came flooding back as I lay in my hammock sipping my beer. Perhaps it was time for me to show that loyalty to Cambodia. I looked along the white sand-coloured beach and thought, 'I really am at home here.'

EPILOGUE

HAVING DECIDED to turn Reuters down and stay in Cambodia, I continued to run the TV Channels. Even though I was only on a 1-year contract, I stayed with Oknha for 10 years. I also created a Khmer language TV channel in the United States for the Cambodian diaspora and helped start a 24-hour Khmer language news channel in Phnom Penh.

Having worked at the highest level of international news with Reuters, I couldn't see myself running a 24-hour news channel in Cambodia where covering news could be challenging.

After planning the 24-hour news channel, I left to start my PR consultancy. It was Cambodia's first dedicated PR company and numbered some of the country's blue-chip companies as clients.

"You can stay on as a consultant," Oknha suggested as I handed in my resignation. And I did for a few years before being asked to go to Myanmar.

While running Oknha's TV channels, we achieved much - among them quite a few firsts. We were the first to put proper news on air (replacing the BBC bulletins that were ripped off, translated and broadcast complete with UK presenters), the first to do a satellite feed TO Cambodia when Cambodia' signed an MOU with WTO, the first to do regular satellite feeds FROM Cambodia - with the broadcast of the United Nations-sponsored Khmer Rouge tribunal, the first to buy and produce 'format' programs such as Deal or No Deal and Hole in the Wall, the first to do international team kickboxing and the first to stage international concerts with artists such as Michael Learns to Rock and Ronan Keating.

Most projects went to plan. Others didn't.

For example, there was a time when we bought Euro 2004 and inspired by the gambling habits of our kickboxing fans, we decided to extend 'telephonic betting' to our sporting events. In doing this, we asked our TV viewers to predict the winners of European football matches.

"Do you know your football?
Are you a football expert?
If so, you could stand a chance to win a 5000 US dollar prize!
All you have to do is to predict the winner of our live and exclusive European football matches!
Votes must be in by half-time for each match!
Choose A or Choose B!
Make sure you send us your texts!"

There was nothing at all wrong with the promo. But

there was something wrong with the telephone shortcodes we had assigned.

"Stop the contest! Stop the betting!" I was instructed by one of the marketing managers at the mobile phone company.

"Why!?! What!?!" I replied.

"The shortcode for team B is connected to Oknha's number!"

"But we've been promoting this contest for days. We can't just stop it."

"He's getting thousands and thousands of texts an hour!"

Being European football, the matches took place late at night, starting at eleven o'clock and ending at about one in the morning. By nine o'clock the next day, the mobile phone company would collate the results and count the number of participants. After the first night's matches, there had been tens of thousands of entrants. For the second night's games, there had been even more.

As it turned out, Oknha had been on a business trip to Australia and had been on a different number. He had only just returned the night before. As soon as he arrived and turned on his phone, thousands of messages began pouring in, making his phone unusable. He had to turn it off again.

"Can't we just change the number?" I asked.

"Can," came the reply.

And with that, the SMS contest continued, and Oknha could go about his nocturnal affairs uninterrupted by football fans sending him a barrage of texts.

On another occasion, we brought a rapper to Cambodia – whose name shall remain nameless because of the sensitivities involved!

"Song very big! Local singer sings his song!" I was told by Sreng. "We should bring the singer to Cambodia."

I dutifully chased down the promoter – only to discover that it was not Michael and his company Midas this time. It was an agent we hadn't used before.

It would be a track show, which they called Minus 1 in the concert trade, and it was a fairly flexible technical rider. Though he did need a stretch limousine – which I couldn't help thinking was overkill on the increasingly cluttered, moto-laden boulevards of Phnom Penh.

Promoting concerts had become a routine for us now. Find the local version of the song, edit it to the original music video, play it a lot on TV and support it with news stories and sell tickets. We did as we always had done and sold about three thousand tickets for the indoor stadium we used on this occasion.

The ninety-minute set went off without a hitch, and the artist left the stage when it was over. But he never said goodbye. He just strolled off, leaving a bemused crowd wondering whether the concert had finished or if there would be an encore.

After about 10 minutes of nothing happening and a crowd getting increasingly impatient, I went backstage.

"I need to speak to him," I told the artist's manager.

"No. He's resting," the manager replied stoically.

"Resting?" I replied, exasperated. "I have three thousand people out there wondering whether the concert is over or if there will be an encore."

"He's finished," the manager responded.

"Well, he needs to say goodbye, do an encore or do something. Thousands of people are out there wondering whether they should stay or go. I need to clear the venue. He needs to say goodbye or something."

Begrudgingly the artist went out, did an encore, shouted goodbye rather rudely, and then left.

After the concert, he went to a party. I left him with our team.

The following day I awoke to a call from Bora.

"Sir! Sir! We have a big problem!"

"What now?" I asked nervously.

"Our singer offended Oknha," Bora explained. "Oknha wants a photo, and the manager refuse."

"Oh!"

"Now Oknha want artists to go airport on *moto*. He wants to cancel the stretch limousine. How can I do?"

I considered the damage that complying with Oknha's wishes would do to the country's reputation.

"Oknha order me cancel VIP terminal too," was the last thing Bora said as he rang off.

I called Oknha.

"Oknha, I know you're angry, but I think we need to reconsider," I reasoned. "I don't mind if you take away the limousine, but at least let him go to the airport on a bus. And as for the VIP terminal, letting him go through the normal channels will cause chaos. People will be asking for photos and autographs, and then security and immigration will have a headache. The head of immigration will probably call you to complain. You will regret it."

"Hmmm, hmmm, hmmm," Oknha replied.

"Besides, he'll talk when he gets back to Los Angeles. We want him to say good things about Cambodia so that other celebrities want to come here too. It'll be good for the country," I continued. "If you send him off on a *moto*, he'll tell everybody he was mistreated. We don't want that."

"OK. Cancel the limousine. Send him to the airport on a bus," Oknha replied. "No air conditioning!"

And we did. Our guest was last seen making his sweaty way through the VIP terminal.

So, even though Oknha and I might have had our differences together, we were a pretty good team. We achieved a lot.

And as for Cambodia, perhaps it was the tonic I desperately needed after spending almost a decade traipsing the world's warzones and hotspots.

On one occasion, I asked our head of engineering, Sothea, to digitise my old Reuters tapes. They were pal beta, and I worried they would deteriorate and be lost forever. They showed wars in Bosnia, Kosovo, and Congo-Brazzaville and the results of civil strife in places like Congo-Kinshasa and Albania. Some of the footage showed market massacres and dead bodies and the like. It also showed me being blown up in a TV building in Sarajevo and rescuing Taras from angry Serbs in Kosovo.

"Sir! Sir! We should show your tape to all staff. It will inspire them! It will motivate them!" Sothea suggested.

"No! Absolutely not!" I replied, refusing Sothea's request. "That is my personal archive."

The truth was that the Khmers had been through so much more than I ever had. Who was I to lecture them on hardship and strife? Besides, I just wanted them to remember me as the crazy pointy-nosed *barang* who brought international concerts and team kickboxing to Cambodia. That was good enough for me. I just hope it was good enough for them too.

WHAT HAPPENED NEXT?

Having successfully set up TV channels in Cambodia, Glen is head-hunted to set up a TV Channel in Myanmar as Yangon gets to grips with a short-lived new democracy. But the question *really* is, is Glen being used to secure investment? Or is he a fall guy for the local shareholder?

Or can he duplicate the successes he experienced in Cambodia?

They've got the guns

I WAS A NERVOUS WRECK. I had been told that the Myanmar authorities didn't like journalists.

In fact, I had been stopped from entering Myanmar before when I had a meeting arranged to talk about a television project. At the time, I was with an outfit called TVnewsweb. We were touting the benefits of delivering news stories via the internet instead of satellite. The Myanmar Ministry of Information had expressed interest and had agreed to meet - until they realised that I was an ex-Reuters journalist.

"There is nothing I can do," the official exclaimed over the phone. "Journalists are not allowed here."

And so it was that I sent an erstwhile deputy in my stead. He reported that when he arrived, immigration checked sheets of paper to see if he was on a banned list. He wasn't. He was let through. He held his meetings with Myanmar's Ministry of Information. However, nothing came of them, and he returned with a bunch of happy snaps and souvenirs.

It was 2000 when my colleague visited Myanmar, and that was 13 years ago. Now it was 2013, and the country had allegedly opened up to the point that former journalists such as myself were now allowed in - or so I was told. The next thirty minutes would determine whether this was the case or not. I gulped as I stood in a group of businessmen and businesswomen. We all had one thing in common - we were waiting for a visa.

The arrivals hall was sparse and cold. There was little in the way of furnishings except for some metallic bench seating. They were uninviting - and certainly not conducive to lounging or resting. And, by the look of it, my fellow travellers were not interested in creature comforts. They were on tenterhooks. They just wanted that all-important full-page stamp in their passport that allowed them to enter Myanmar. I waited nervously for the same.

It had been about fifteen minutes since I handed my passport and paperwork to a surly-faced immigration officer. I pondered going over to the metallic bench seating to sit and wait. I thought better of it. I didn't want to risk missing my turn with the immigration officers.

"Passpot!" the officer had demanded.

I handed it over.

"Invitation!"

I handed that over too.

"Company!"

I then handed him a letter of incorporation from the company I was coming to meet and my own company's incorporation agreements. I watched as the receiving officer passed them to another officer for checking before being passed to another for stamping. Only then, after my passport and papers had run the gauntlet of immigration officers, would I be let through.

"Felgate!" I heard an immigration official bark. My name was announced, emphasising the final e as 'ey'. I had become 'Felgatey!' instead of 'Felgate".

I stepped forward, breaking off from the throng of anxious businessmen and businesswomen as I did so. I half-expected to be taken off into a private room to be grilled about my past endeavours as a journalist. I braced myself for what would come next.

"Passport photo?" the immigration official demanded.

"Ah yes," I responded, digging into my laptop bag for a photo. I handed it over and watched the immigration officer clip it to an official application form.

"Enjoy your stay," the immigration officer smiled.

I was through!

It was now 2013. I had been sitting at my desk twiddling my thumbs in my Public Relations agency office in Cambodia when the email came in. It was from a Singaporean attached to a Myanmar businessman with a digital TV licence. A supplier I used to do business with while running Cambodian TV channels had put my name forward. I was there on an exploratory visit.

I had been invited to someone connected to the Burmese Army's Psychological Warfare unit. Menacing as it sounded, I was told that it was actually OK. Myanmar was the new darling of the West and East. United States President Barack Obama had even visited in 2012.

Before embarking on this particular foray, I did my own due diligence. I checked the United States government's website to ensure the licence holder was not on the Specially Designated Nationals And Blocked Persons List (SDN), the United States government's list for whom sanctions apply. As it happened, he wasn't. He passed on that score. However, unbeknown to me, he was the public face of the Myanmar Army's 'Directorate of Public Relation and Psychology Warfare of the Defence Chief of General Staff' - as it was spelt on the licence. The licence holder's job was to run a series of nationwide digital TV channels by providing programs and production. He was effectively a TV arms dealer - the one commissioned to buy programs and try to achieve some sales on behalf of the military. But he wasn't an SDN.

And so it was that I bounded out into the arrivals hall of Yangon International Airport to see a stout Myanmar man in what appeared to be a checkered skirt holding a placard with my name on it aloft.

"Mr. Glen?" the man asked.

I nodded.

"You come. You come," the Myanmar man ordered in a gruff baritone before marching through the throng of Western businessmen and businesswomen. He adjusted his skirt-like *longyi* as he strode.

As he marched out into the sunlight, he shot a wad of blood-red betel juice onto the pavement and marched on. He led me past battered white Probox taxis to the airport's car park. There he marched determinedly to a black Mitsubishi Pajero. It looked like it had seen better days and needed a wash - as did my host.

"OK, OK! You come," my host ordered through teeth stained blood-red by the betel juice.

Once I was settled in the back of the car, my host - who appeared to be the licence holder's driver - moved off.

"OK, OK! Yangon..." my driver announced.

"Very nice," I replied.

"OK, OK!" he responded again.

And that was that. I appeared to have exhausted my driver's capacity for introductory small talk. I sat back and took stock of my surroundings.

Yangon was big and leafy. The main thoroughfares were well constructed and planned, as expected in China or a major European city. They were a far cry from the poky, dirt tracks and pot-holed boulevards that I had become used to in Phnom Penh.

Battered vehicles trundled along, and although they were not as dilapidated as they were in Phnom Penh, they were outdated and presumably out of production. The prevalent car on the road appeared to be a Toyota Probox - which was always invariably white and worn down. Most steering wheels were on the right - and they drove on the right too. There were absolutely no motorbikes.

"Where are the motorbikes?" I asked my driver.

"No!" came the reply. My driver looked at me in the rear-view mirror and spat another wad of betel juice through the open car window. He returned his attention to the highway.

"Shwedagon!" my driver suddenly announced. "Good!"

I looked across to see a golden stupa rising above the skyline. It was situated on a hill and stood out from the sea of grey and brick buildings that made up Yangon's skyline.

"Impressive," I agreed.

"Good!" my driver announced again before spitting more betel juice into the street.

We were nearing the centre of downtown Yangon. There, I was transported to days gone by with the appearance of old British administrative buildings. Architecturally, I had stepped back in time. The customs houses, post offices and Churches were relics of days gone by. They still retained their majesty - but looked worn. It was like being on an old 1920s film set.

Old colonial buildings poked out from behind sprawling shrubs and massive trees, and foliage was everywhere. Vines and hedges overtook the homes and gardens, giving everything a vibrant natural feel. However, the buildings appeared mildewed, worn and dilapidated.

Despite their dishevelled appearance, the old architecture added an authentic colonial air to the place. It also added to the mystique. I had the feeling that anything could happen at any time. I had the feeling of being somewhere unique.

On the sidewalks were knick-knack stalls where people sold their possessions. Some looked authentically antique, while others were distinctly kitsch. There were tea shops with rickety wooden tables and shiny plastic stools. Next to them were the booksellers selling out-of-print classics by George Orwell and other established authors.

George Orwell had been a Burma policeman. He had penned the book Burmese Days, which was loosely based on his experiences in up-country Myanmar. It was a classic, and the booksellers hoped to capitalise on his literary success.

Driving through downtown Yangon, I watched Myanmar men and women coming and going. They strode along the pavements with dainty steps restricted by their everyday attire. The men were dressed like my driver. They wore the traditional *longyi* and sandals or flip-flops. Women wore coloured wrap-around skirts with matching embroidered tops. They appeared to be proud of their unique, unusual fashion statements.

Almost all of the women had a smidgen of *thanaka* on each cheek. Thanaka was a form of make-up made from the bark of a tree that was ground and mixed with water to form a paste. Once applied, it appeared cream in colour. Myanmar women believe wearing *thanaka* would clear the skin of blemishes, I was later informed. It provided sun protection too.

As I admired my strangely new surroundings, we turned into barracks. A guard with Military Police insignia stared suspiciously at me as he questioned my driver. His manner was surly to the point of being rude. He lifted the barrier reluctantly. I appeared to have made it past military officialdom for the second time that day.

The military compound I now entered consisted of crumbling barracks and a red-brick building. There was a parade ground and what appeared to be a motor pool with jeeps and flat-bed army trucks. Off to the side were pieces of heavy artillery. They languished in the sun. Camouflage netting had been casually draped over the barrel of a gun, indicating that they were in temporary storage.

My driver escorted me into the building via an approach already flooded with pools of muddy water. I stepped delicately over the puddles and thought that, with Myanmar's annual rainy season still a month away, the muddy brown puddles were a product of poor drainage rather than the country's harsh elements.

Stepping across the threshold, my driver encouraged me

to remove my shoes. It appeared to be standard practice. A line of flip-flops and slip-ons greeted visitors at the entrance.

The ground floor of the two-storey building was being used as a warehouse. There were barrels and drums of cable scattered across the floor. Upstairs was an open plan area with sickly green walls and wobbly Chinese-made chairs and tables. Sliding glass doors divided compartments of open-plan office space.

"Ah, Glen, good to see you," my Singaporean host said, holding his hand out in greeting as he rose from a wobbly wooden table. "I'm Winston. Thank you for coming. I'm glad you made it. I'll fill you in on our contact, U Kyaw Kyaw."

The Singaporean then spent the next thirty minutes expounding on the virtues of our would-be partner U Kyaw Kyaw.

"His name is Kyaw Kyaw. Kyaw is pronounced 'chore' here. You use first and last names, so it's always Kyaw Kyaw. And it is always U Kyaw Kyaw. U in Myanmar is like Sir."

"For heaven's sake, always use U," Winston pleaded.

"This is starting to sound very familiar," I smiled as I recalled my arrival in Cambodia over a decade before.

"...so, he was educated in Singapore and has a brother close to the military," Winston said, wrapping up the briefing. "With the US lifting sanctions, Myanmar is accepted by the world. And I'm helping U Kyaw Kyaw relaunch his TV. I think it has potential. I hope you can help."

"But it is owned by the military, no?" I asked.

"Yes, but since Obama's visit and lifting sanctions, that is all OK. Now it is all about engagement."

United States President Barack Obama made history in

2012 when he became the first American president to visit Myanmar. His visit effectively gave the green light for foreign investment and engagement. And, now, as a result, foreign mobile phone companies and other corporations were falling over themselves to get a piece of the action in what was being described as 'the world's last frontier'. They were hoping to have a 'first mover advantage'.

It was then that the local shareholder U Kyaw Kyaw walked in. He sported a large toothy smile and a pleasant manner. He was about fifty, and he was very slim. He didn't wear the traditional *longyi* dress. Instead, he wore smart-casual trousers and a short sleeve shirt.

"Mr. Glen, I would like to take this opportunity to warmly welcome you to our country," the local shareholder said. "We warmly welcome you to our humble TV channel too. We hope that you can help us. We hope you can do what you did in Cambodia for us."

U Kyaw Kyaw referenced my launching and running Cambodia's number 1 commercial television network. He had apparently seen my CV. He did not reference my previous experience working as a journalist for Reuters.

As I looked around, I could see frail desks and plastic chairs. There were no control rooms, cameras, or edit packs in evidence. Instead, a few people sat wearing headphones and peered intently at programs on dusty TV sets. They appeared to be taking notes.

"This is our team," U Kyaw Kyaw said proudly. "They are translating programs for our channels."

As I looked closer, I saw that the programs were a mixture of Chinese, Thai and Indian. 'The team' sat scribbling on grubby bits of paper as they worked. The pieces of paper were then attached to a clipboard. A supervisor seemed to wander among them.

"We are a very diverse country, Mr. Glen," U Kyaw Kyaw continued. "Our audience has many varied tastes. They like Indian, Chinese and Thai. They also like Korean."

"That is very similar to Cambodia," I replied. "It seems that you have the same tastes."

"Are there any big 'no-no's. Anything we cannot broadcast," I asked.

"There are some stipulations and regulations in our licence agreement, but they are mainly about Myanmar culture. But we are fairly free to broadcast most things," U Kyaw Kyaw replied. "We are a very tolerant people."

The Myanmar people tolerated most people and cultures – except for the Rohingya. That is where they drew the line. Recent reports of violence against the Muslim Rohingya in Rakhine State to the west of Myanmar had been reported. I decided to ask about it.

"What about the Rohingya issue?" I asked. "Will it affect stability?"

"Ah, yes, 'the people who call themselves Rohingya'", U Kyaw Kyaw replied. He wasn't being facetious; he was following orders. "'The people who called themselves Rohynga' is how the government asks us to refer to this particular ethnic group. After all, they do not really exist. They are Bengalis who have drifted across the border and claimed land. We don't need to worry about them. We are an entertainment network, not news."

"But we do need to broadcast certain programs and events brought to us by the military," U Kyaw Kyaw added.

"After all, they do hold twenty-five per cent of the seats...and they do have the guns."

As U Kyaw Kyaw spoke, I recalled the camouflaged heavy artillery lying in wait in the car park.

"Anyway, when I saw your profile, I thought you might just be crazy enough to do this..." Winston then interjected, changing the subject quickly.

"Well, it'll certainly be a challenge," I replied, smiling. "With or without the guns."

I suddenly had a sense of déjà vu.

Evacuated from Libya, blown up in a TV building during the Bosnian war, handed over to rebels after a coup in Sierra Leone, Glen Felgate's life has been one big adventure after another.

The son of a British oil worker, Glen was brought up in Libya, Kuwait and Malaysia, and schooled in England and the United States.

In 1993, aged 30, Glen joined a little-known television news agency called Visnews just before it was acquired by the world's biggest news agency Reuters. Glen covered wars in Bosnia, Kosovo and Africa. He covered the collapse of pyramid schemes in Albania and regularly visited the annual World Economic Forum in Davos.

After spending almost ten years covering the world's hot spots, Glen left Reuters to strike out on his own. Somehow, he found himself in Cambodia where he was invited to set up TV channels for some of the country's wealthiest tycoons.

Glen is currently living in Phnom Penh where he is still involved with the media and writes books.

Contacts and Links

Website: www.glenfelgateauthor.com

Facebook:
www.facebook.com/glenfelgateauthor
www.facebook.com/glen.felgate

Twitter:
https://www.twitter.com/felgateglen

Email: glen.felgate@gmail.com

If you'd like to chat with the author and other memoir authors and readers, do join the friendly, fun Facebook group, We Love Memoirs.

https://www.facebook.com/groups/welovememoirs/